IMAGINE MEETING HIM

IMAGINE MEETING HIM

SOUL-STIRRING ENCOUNTERS WITH THE SON OF GOD

ROBERT RASMUSSEN

MULTNOMAH PUBLISHERS
Sisters, Oregon

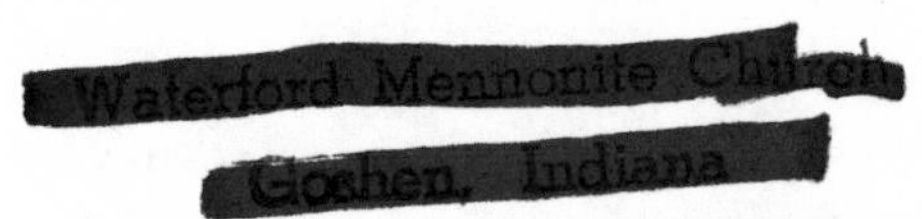

IMAGINE MEETING HIM
published by Multnomah Publishers, Inc.

International Standard Book Number: 1-57673-251-7

Published in association with the literary agency of Alive Communications, 1465 Kelly Johnson Blvd., Suite 320, Colorado Springs, CO 80920.

Cover painting: *Woman of Samaria* by Bloch (SuperStock, Inc.)
Cover design by D[2] DesignWorks

Printed in the United States of America

For information:
Multnomah Publishers, Inc.
Post Office Box 1720
Sisters, Oregon 97759

Library of Congress Cataloging-in-Publication Data:
Rasmussen, Robert, 1952–
Imagine meeting Him/by Robert Rasmussen.
p. cm.
Includes indexes.
ISBN 1–57673–251–7 (paper)
1. Jesus Christ—Meditations. I. Title.
BT306.4.R37 1998
232–dc21
97–36551
CIP

98 99 00 01 02 03 04 05 06 07 — 10 9 8 7 6 5 4 3 2 1

To my parents,
Gordon and June Rasmussen

For your love of God's Word and consistent obedience to it,
for your example of perseverance through trials and
graciousness when wronged,
and for introducing your four children to the Savior,
I thank and honor you.

CONTENTS

PART FOUR

IN THE DISSIPATING MISTS OF A NEW DAWN

ACKNOWLEDGMENTS

Allow me to publicly thank some of the key people who have helped this book become a reality. My thanks to:

- Chuck Kelley, for encouraging me to write;
- Scott Sterling, Roger McNichols Jr., and Russ Lambert—faithful messengers along the way;
- Kathy Yanni for steering this book, Dan Benson for harboring it, Lisa Lauffer and Carol Bartley for polishing it;
- my teammates in Africa who have enriched my life: Joash and Esther Mutua, Lee and Sandy Weiss, Don and Pam Kearby, Jim and Sue DeVries, Rick and Debbie Cruse, Stan and Donna Downes;
- my mainstay, best friend, and wife, Lyn, without whose love and cheerleading I likely would have faltered long ago.

I also want to thank you, my reader/friend, for sharing this pilgrimage with me.

Bob Rasmussen
Nairobi, Kenya

A Prayer

May any who speak
be inaudible,
that Jesus alone be heard.

May any who sing
be invisible,
that Christ alone be seen.

May any who write
be unnoticeable,
that he alone be praised.

PREFACE

Imagine Meeting Him

Meeting Jesus Christ is the single most important event of any and every life. The person who has met Christ is complete even if everything else in life goes wrong...even if that person never produces anything else of significance.

The person who has not met him, no matter what else he or she accomplishes, is empty. Not just empty by comparison but, on the scales of eternity, *absolutely* empty.

How can I say that? Because of who Jesus is. Jesus is music to a concert. He is air to a deep breath. He is gravity to falling. He is life to living.

Try life with Jesus, and then attempt it without him. You'll see what I mean.

What does it mean to meet Christ? Two things, as I see it.

First, meeting Christ is an Event. It is to encounter him. To embrace and be embraced. It is to grasp the basic essence of Jesus and to understand with childlike simplicity what he has done for you and its importance to your life and destiny.

You meet Christ when you place your trust in him as completely as you know how and, as a result, receive the irrevocable gift of eternal life. It's an Event in which you begin a journey with him determined to stay with him all the way to the end, no matter what.

Meeting Christ is also a Process. It's the journey itself, the adventure of traveling with him over whatever terrain you encounter. It's the adventure that warms up in time and blasts off in eternity.

This Process calls you to endure a full cycle of experiences with Christ, as many times and to whatever extent he asks…

In the Morning's Warmth of Blooming Friendship

…from the euphoria of discovering for the first time what he's like;

In the Daytime Paths of Deeper Companionship

…to the challenging joy of getting to know him more intimately;

In the Solitude of the Night Watches

…from the loneliness and pain of understanding and experiencing his suffering;

In the Dissipating Mists of a New Dawn

…to the clearing of the fog of carnality and mortality in order to finally see Christ as he truly is and know him as completely as he has known you.

When we look at the events of Jesus' earthly life, it is impossible to miss the fact that he desires us to meet him. He does not run from relationships.

On the contrary, he placed people at the top of his agenda, far above programs or campaigns. Rich but empty people. Diseased but believing people. Demonized people. Poor people. You name it.

So committed was he to encountering and impacting people that he allowed his notoriety to suffer so he could pursue relationships with those who needed him. His popularity often took a beating because people were his program.

Watch the Master in action. At a synagogue, at a funeral. At breakfast on a beach, at a dinner party with a tax collector's questionable cronies. At night with a Pharisee, at high noon with a Samaritan woman. Jesus wanted people to know him. He threw open windows galore so that they (and we) could get an unobstructed view of his true nature.

And notice. He didn't sell salt to a thirsty man. Didn't give fire to a child.

No, Jesus meets each person at his or her point of need. Some need the gentle touch, others firm. Some lack encouragement, others clear guidance. Some crave nothing more than attention and friendship, others a view of his eternal power.

Would you like to meet dozens of people who actually saw Jesus face to face? Woven together, their stories tell a single tale: Get to know him.

We have their tale. It turns out to be a story of friendship with Jesus Christ. This friendship is not the easiest, but it's easily the richest. And it's available to anyone who desires it.

Come with me to times and places where Jesus actually was, actually *is*. Come, meet him afresh. Try to discern what he's really like. Feel what it would have been like to be with him.

Lose yourself and your defenses. Shake off your sense of distance from him.

Go back. Go further in. Go closer.

This is not a book of expositions, though plenty of study went into it. Neither is it a book of applications, though you will find a lot of practical truth to consider and act on.

What you hold in your hand is a collection of, for lack of a better term, "imaginations." These stories don't satisfy all the demands of historical accuracy. They don't tie up every logical, chronological, or even theological loose end. They do contain a fair amount of personal opinion.

Would you do something? Don't worry about it.

Be like the believers from Berea (Acts 17:11). They didn't take anybody's word for it. Do the same yourself; go to the Scriptures and dig for your life. And may this book find frequent rest in your lap while you look up from its pages to reflect on new dimensions of your friendship with him. To help you do so, I've provided questions at the end of each vignette in a section called "For Reflection." I invite you to allow these prompters to take you into deeper consideration of your relationship with Christ.

Let the people who met Jesus carry you along with their stories. Let them make you laugh. Or shed a tear with them. But by all means, let them take you further in life's most important adventure.

PART ONE

In the Morning's Warmth of Blooming Friendship

Friendships are like stories. Some are better than others. They have their ups and downs, their tensions and releases, their climaxes and anticlimaxes. Both go through various "chapters" that tell the tale of deepening understanding or intimacy or fun.

Every friendship, like every story, has a beginning—a special time of discovering just what kind of person you have met along your life's journey. The opening chapters of a friendship bring joy. They build your anticipation; they whet your appetite for more:

What is this person interested in?
What abilities and talents are hiding inside, waiting to be discovered?
What kind of relationship could we possibly have? A casual friend ship? Or could this be that deep and true friend I've been hoping for?
What idiosyncrasies do I notice that I would have to put up with? Would I find them interesting or unbearable?
What opinions does this person hold about politics and economics? And do I even care?
What about children and travel? the arts or sports?

These queries coax open the bud of friendship. They can bring a euphoric sense of exploration that transcends age and cultural barriers.

Especially when that new friend is Jesus Christ.

It would be a great loss to miss this getting-acquainted stage of discovering Christ as an exciting new friend. But many do just that. They miss the beginning chapters.

Some who do so never find Christ as their Savior. As a result, they never find him as their Friend either.

But others who miss out on friendship with Christ are Christians. Perhaps they're introduced to Jesus under the heavy hand of duty. They never see him as anyone other than a strict taskmaster with next-to-impossible demands.

Other Christians are taught about a Christ who is forever angry. To them, Jesus is always hopping mad about something bad somebody did.

Still others are given the impression that Jesus is remote—here for a while a long time ago but now basically disinterested. What can anybody discover about a Jesus who's somewhere out in deep space?

Those thoughts nip friendship in the bud. It's the Christian life without any fragrance. It's like viewing a flower garden in black and white.

And it gyps Jesus. Because he's neither a cruel master, a grouch, nor a bore.

That's why we all need to go back time and time again to become reacquainted with the real Jesus as if for the first time. To pay attention to his mannerisms. To listen closely to his words so as to pick up hints of his deeper meaning. To let him impact our lives anew or advise us on one of our other relationships.

Many believers push hard to accomplish good things for Christ. They could rightfully claim hard work and perseverance as their strengths. They could get credit for refusing to tolerate evil. They could receive commendation for enduring hardships without quitting or even growing weary.

If that describes you, you are to be applauded. Jesus is pleased with you.

I can say that on the authority of God's Word, for the Lord Jesus, through his Spirit, commended the church at Ephesus for these very things (Revelation 2:1–3).

But you know where I'm going with this discussion because you know what Jesus added to his words of approval: "Yet I hold this against you: You have forsaken your first love. Remember the height from which you have fallen! Repent and do the things you did at first" (Revelation 2:4–5).

He says (if I may paraphrase liberally and aim it your direction) that he misses the times he used to have with you, sitting as if in a field of thick grass and wildflowers, pulling long-stemmed weeds and chewing on the soft core, looking into the distance, and enjoying your company.

He appreciates your work. But he misses you.

The sun is up. It feels warm and good. Friendship is in the air. Can you feel it?

CHAPTER ONE

IMAGINE HIM NOTICING YOU

It's more than a glance.

It's when the eyes of a significant person fix on you with interest. Maybe that interest says, "I want to get to know you" or "something about you makes you special."

Often, someone significant noticing you can make your heart thump with joy, like the young schoolboy who finally catches the eye of the prettiest girl in his class or the businesswoman who, through long and hard labor, ultimately grabs her supervisor's attention and garners a bonus or promotion.

At other times, such discovery seems our enemy: To be noticed is to be found out. It is to have a light beamed into our preferred cover of darkness.

What would it feel like to have the Son of God notice you? To have his eyes meet yours? To realize he was watching you from a distance?

Imagine it. It happened.

And it's still happening.

SURPRISED BY ACCEPTANCE

I met him in the oddest way.

I'm a loner, you see. Congregating is for hens; that's my philosophy.

But curiosity gets the better of me. I had heard his name many times but thought little of it—probably another eccentric preacher that lonely widows and fickle young people get enamored with for a week or two. But the reports about him persisted...his name kept cropping up. I had even heard some of my clients—level-headed businessmen, intelligent investors—speak of Christ, of wonders a bit too odd to be real, of teachings filled with irony and mystery.

Passing fancy? A good act? Almost positively. But still, I found myself wondering.

So one day I went for the bait. Knowingly, with eyes wide open. *I'll check him out for myself,* I decided.

I wanted to play the observer...from a safe distance. Close enough to see and evaluate...not so close as to be discovered. So I found a perch above the crowd.

Then my plan went haywire. Not only did he notice me but worse still he focused on me. His eyes and words pointed the spotlight on my hide-out: "I want to come to your house."

No, you really don't.

Found out.

How could I have been such a fool? I should have trusted my instincts. Should have ignored him.

Must run. It's my way. Must run. Should run.

But he had stopped, you see. He had shown interest in me. Knew my name. Wanted to come to my house. That touched something in me I just couldn't ignore.

Tentatively at first I climbed down from my self-protection. I let loose of the branch of skepticism. I headed homeward, saying nothing, hearing his footsteps close behind, just beyond my usually cold shoulder.

What is it about this man that makes avoidance seem wrong? Do I feel he knows me—with all my hidden faults, all my shame—yet accepts me? Does he know the kind of person I am? About the number of people I've cheated for years on end? The verbal abuse? He couldn't know how I've gone after those who couldn't afford to sue me.

Or could he? Could he possibly overlook my checkered past and forgive?

He knows those with a religious exterior. He seems to look past their fronts to see what's inside: the selfishness and deceit. Perhaps he sees past my greedy facade, too. Could he know that deep within I really care, that I really want to do what's right?

When I met him, I found myself on the most frightening emotional journey available to anyone: exposed...known...understood.

But I survived, for my guide was the man of all grace.

Luke 19:1–10

FOR REFLECTION: Do I risk coming out of my hiding? In what ways? How does it feel these days?

A Wounded Hero

Picture in your mind's eye a group of two dozen adults.

Now eliminate from your mental scene all who appear insincere, who don't quite look as if they mean what they say.

Next take away all whose features and skin color speak of opportunity or even just a fair chance—those who have privileges because of their race.

You should now have a significantly reduced number of people, all of whom live day to day in a kind of uphill climb.

Next remove all those who in most parts of the world hold certain undeniable privileges: the men.

Your remnant now consists of a small group of survivors. By records that too few keep, they are heroes.

Look into the eyes of these remaining women. In which pair of eyes do you see the most apparent fatigue? Which eyes are set deeply with the heaviness of sin, failure, and disappointment?

She's the one: the wounded hero no one would bother to give a second glance. No one sees any value in her other than a body to be used and discarded.

Her earlier dreams have proven illusory. To defend herself against further disappointment, she has subconsciously ceased pondering the future.

Many men have broken their promises to her. Each one in his own convincing way wooed her with suave verbiage about how wonderful their lives together would be.

She has been trusting. Too trusting. And as a result, she has known many men. Fed up, she's nevertheless unable to break the cycle, not strong enough to go it alone. She has continued to enter into unsatisfying relationships and even now finds herself in yet another dead-end arrangement from which she has nothing to gain.

Her parents raised her within the sphere of deep religious tradition. She believed in God and sought to worship him. But she found it a largely formal pursuit.

Almost daily she thought of the promise of the Savior, of what a breakthrough his appearance would be for her people, of how much closer God would seem after waiting so long in silence.

She felt a longing deep within her. Call it a thirst. Her soul yearned for a deep drink that would bring lingering satisfaction, one that would see her through the fractured relationships and the days of hard work that promised nothing more than survival.

The endless round of chores brought her in the heat of the day to the well to draw water. There was cooking and cleaning to do if she wanted to keep her man from getting angry.

Little did she know that the Savior himself would rest at that very well. (How could she have known that Jesus is adept at being available to those who are hurting and longing for his aid?) How close she was to her life's answer! How close to hope! How near was the quenching drink that her thirsty soul craved.

But how high the obstacles before she could encounter him. How hopeless for her to think she could recognize him and, even if she did, reach out to him.

It was impossible, for she was the wrong kind. The categories of society had rendered her twice removed from him. They were together at the same well but like two planets in nonintersecting orbits.

She was the wrong race. Her culture, her beliefs, her traditions, her language, her homeland—all were different from his.

And she was the wrong gender. Living under social mores as inflexible as stone, she was on the wrong side of a granite wall of ostracism. He stood on the side where men could interact freely, exchanging ideas and inquiring about beliefs and spiritual hopes. She stood beyond the range of even seeing or hearing such openness. She could only know what might trickle down by happenstance.

Well accustomed to her isolation, she went about her business, not even considering the possibility that through simple conversation she'd find the one who could bring light into her dark hovel. Words, even if they were hers to use, could not reach as high as the class of man who happened to cross her path that day.

And how unfortunate. It might have been a meeting to change a life. It could have rolled back the years and soothed the hurts of five failed marriages. It might have removed the salt from a hundred wounds, the sting from a thousand broken promises. It might have brought hope to a life that had given up hoping.

If there had been even the remotest possibility that this man would for some unknown reason shatter every tradition…

If for no other reason than the writing of a grand story the Lord could have known of her thirst and found a way to give her a drink…

…wouldn't it have been a wonder to behold?

Wasn't it?

The enigmatic Jewish man did the unthinkable. When the Samaritan woman came to draw water, he said to her, "Will you give me a drink?"

Seeing her thirst, he asked for water.

And the rest is her story.

John 4:5–42

FOR REFLECTION: Do I think that Jesus cannot notice my longings?

"HE SEEMED TO KNOW ME"

Nathan, seeker after truth, to Joseph, my good friend, whom I trust.

I have some terrific news to write: I've met Christ. That's right. *The* Christ.

Let me back up. You know already that for some time I've been reading the Scriptures. I've kept it a personal thing. In fact, you're the only one I've told. Well, the more I've studied the more intrigued I've become with Christ. He strikes me as such a compelling and mysterious figure.

Last week, Wednesday it was, I was out in a little hideaway I've made in the grove of trees behind my house. It's a completely private place that no one knows about. Perhaps uncharacteristically, I was praying. The gist of my prayer was, "Christ, if you're real, reveal yourself to me."

Next day the strangest thing happened. I ran into a guy named Philip whom I haven't seen in over a year. Actually he ran into me—saw me in town, came running up and, as if he knew about my spiritual search, said, "We've found him. Come and see."

Everything inside me bristled with resistance. My spiritual inquisitiveness wasn't for public consumption. Who was Philip to presume I'd even care about Christ? And what would make me think that the one I sought would be someone you could "come and see" like a new attraction in town?

But I went anyway. Joseph, it was amazing. As I approached him, he had his back toward me. But he seemed to know I was coming. He turned around as if on cue, looked me right in the eye, and announced, "Here's a man who wouldn't deceive you."

Under normal circumstances I would have written the guy off as a nut. But my usual defensive comeback didn't come to mind. (All I could manage was a weak, "How do you know me?") He looked at me as if he knew what was really going on inside.

That's not all. He said he had noticed me when I was praying in the trees. My friend, no one knew I was out there or what I was doing. How could he have seen me when I was all alone?

All I can say is that the light went on. I've been groping for insight for months, but somehow in the presence of the person himself, it all came together. It's him, Joseph. I'm sure of it.

I've debated whether to share this other matter with you, but I guess I'll go ahead. I was obviously bowled over by his knowing about my secret prayers and all. But he went on to say something I still don't understand: "You'll see greater things than these. I say to you, you will see the heavens opened, and the angels of God ascending and descending on the Son of Man."

See what I mean? What do you make of it? I feel like he already knows me. He knows my secret past. Could he know my future as well?

As I said, Joseph, you've got to come and see this guy.

All for now,
Nathan

John 1:43–51

FOR REFLECTION: How would I react if I discovered that Jesus knew me inside and out, past and future?

A LONG HOPE

Some of us spend our whole lives waiting for the final chapter,

...like the last chord that resolves the tension in a mysterious concerto,

...like the final piece of evidence that solves a puzzling whodunit.

Such was the experience of a man who had given his life to God's work. Though religion was his occupation, he was not a "professional" in the derogatory sense of the term. He was truly devout, a lover of God.

For years he had greeted each morning with the same persisting query: *Is it today? I'm tired. I want to go to my rest. Is it today you will fulfill your promise?*

A faithful life but unfulfilled.

Because of the promise, he had developed over the years a keen sense of observation. Would it be one of the great teachers on the east side he had heard about? A brilliant young student perhaps? (He had heard of one bright prospect who had memorized the entire Torah.) How about a master craftsman? Or a musician?

No, surely it would be a priest, soaring through the ranks, holding a faultless pedigree.

At times the promise threatened to become a curse. *Did I really hear God's voice, or am I just flattering myself? Is it wishful thinking so I can boast to my colleagues? Has it become the senile obsession of an old man? Oh God, why not today?! Release me.*

Hope was fueled only by the sheer greatness of the promise: that he would personally meet the world's Savior.

On a day when the yearning had never been greater, his soul was strangely stirred with expectancy.

He had always observed the crowds. Always watched. But today, with particular alertness he scanned those entering the outer courts. He searched the halls and the stairways for anyone with that look of destiny, anyone whose face triggered an internal response in his soul.

He looked…and looked.

Maybe not. I'm a fool.

Sighing disappointedly, he reeled around…and there stood before him a young couple. His glance moved from the chiseled face of the father to the youthful smile of the mother. His eyes drifted casually to the smooth countenance of their baby.

Then it happened. Instead of what he had often seen—eyes closed in sleep or wandering with curiosity—this infant's eyes were fixed alertly on his own.

Intuitively the old man knew.

Not a priest. Not a teacher. Not even a prophet. But a baby. A baby!

His aged arms reached out…trembling.

As he held the child, he knew his waiting was over. His life was entering the passageway. He could rest at last. Faithful, yes…and now fulfilled.

Released to death by a child just born. Cradling in his arms his own Creator. Offering a prayer of sacrifice for the one who would offer up his own life. For a moment, holding God.

O Lord, how could I, so unworthy, have a part in such a life as this?

God has loved him; kings have produced him.

An angel named him; a virgin bore him.

Satan fears him; the world will worship him.

And I…I have held him.

Luke 2:21–35

FOR REFLECTION: What can I learn from my season of "hope unfulfilled"?

CHAPTER TWO

IMAGINE HIM TOUCHING YOU

When you consider who he was, compared with who we are,
 the glory of his past, with the shame of ours—
When you remember that he merits the worship of all the world's kings
 and the obedience of all heaven's angels—
If you were able to comprehend the power of one word of his mouth
 or the impact of one millisecond of his attention,
And if you could conceive of
 the strength of his personality as he walks into a crowded room,
 the spine-tingling force of his passing, even at a distance,
 or the compelling appeal of his physical presence,
You would share with me the awe of the words,
 "Jesus stretched out his hand and *touched...*"

FRIENDS

As an eager rooster trumpets the impending dawn, the sun peeks over rooftops silhouetted against a canvas of yellows and oranges.

Flowers in bloom begin to show off their radiant plumage in the spotlight of the first rays. A nearby fountain splashes with explosions of glistening light.

But all of this is for others to see, for you live in a world of darkness. The doorway of sight has been permanently sealed shut without even a trickle of light seeping through a crack.

If only you could get that touch—the touch of the one who, so they say, can heal. The great one from whom power flows. "He even brings the dead to life."

To see. That would be like life to me.

Friends come. They've decided to do something about your "case." They're taking you to Jesus. Could today's dawn be the last colorless one?

They wipe their hands clean, brush off their sleeves. "Here you are. Now Jesus will touch you."

And so he does. But not as you'd expected. Instead, he clasps your hand in his in a firm and manly way. Nothing effeminate or insipid. With a strong grasp he leads you away from the others.

"Hey, where's he going with our poor blind friend?"

He's touched me, but I don't see anything.

Together you walk—hand in hand, stride for stride—like two friends.

Yes, he will tend to your eyes. He'll even do it with special care. Take special time.

But for now, he's giving you something more.

So often when you've walked, you've walked alone. Even when you've misjudged the path and stumbled on a stone, others have stood at a distance…watching, whispering ("Oh, tsk, poor thing…"), unwilling to walk with you. *(Why doesn't someone help me? Are they afraid to touch me?)*

So Jesus gives more than you expect, more than your friends had hoped to brag about. "Come, let's walk together, off by ourselves, and you'll find that in the end you will be whole. Your eyes will see…and so will your heart."

Then the walk comes naturally to an end. You've received the touch of companionship. Dignity gripped your life as Jesus grasped your hand.

Somehow his final words are altogether fitting: "Don't go back to the crowds." As if to say, "You are my special friend. You're not a spectacle for the thrill seekers. You're a person of value and worth. Go your way in the confidence of our friendship. The crowds will know in time that you can see."

Okay, Lord, it's still a bit hazy, but I'm beginning to see what you mean.

Mark 8:22–26

FOR REFLECTION: How can I accept the dignity of my daily stroll with Christ even though I feel so unworthy?

RISK REWARDED

It used to be that when Reuben returned from a trip the children would run into his arms, his infectious belly laugh rolling through the house all the way to the back bedroom. It wouldn't be long before he was completely absorbed in reunion: cuddling the smallest, wrestling the oldest, and later, when alone, sharing with me the high points or disappointments of his journey. His zest for life made him seem invincible.

Perhaps that's why his illness caught us all by surprise.

I couldn't bear widowhood. I'd rather die myself than be without Reuben.

But death did not visit him. At least not in the normal sense. Our lot was a kind of living death: chronic disease. My dear husband was left on earth but removed from us who loved him, separated from us by a great gulf of awkwardness and empty wishes.

His illness robbed us of his playfulness. Of his laughter.

Friends withdrew. Even our own children couldn't bear to be with him very often. It hurt so.

I missed his touch most of all. At night I longed for his caress.

It was so different. I just wanted him back again the way he used to be.

Then the tide turned.

I was with Reuben the day he reached out in desperation. The previous weeks had led to a crescendo of despair. His will seemed to forsake him.

But then the oddest coincidence. Reuben heard of one who told of a divine "kingdom." *What strange talk.* Word of spiritual restoration and physical healing spread curiosity and even hope throughout the colony of despair in which Reuben dwelled.

Something was different that Sunday morning I visited him.

Something was back: the sparkle in his eye that had always served as a precursor to some crazy dream. *Are my feelings deceiving me?*

A faint smile curved the corners of his mouth. "Come with me, dear."

Something is *different.*

"Where are we going?"

"There may be some hope."

The journey we shared…I can't possibly describe it. I held him up, but somehow Reuben really supported me. This journey was our pilgrimage of faith to meet the one who spoke, as they say, like no other.

I had never seen my husband so broken—and yet so intent. *Is there a strength in brokenness?*

When Christ's eyes fell on Reuben's shriveled frame, faith burst forth: "If you are willing, you can make me clean."

Christ's smile shone into the heart of my beloved and melted my fears. His strong hands embraced Reuben's contaminated flesh without hesitation, as if he had so touched a thousand other outcasts.

And then the words came, the words that changed us forever, the words that have healed my own life a hundred times since: "I am willing. Be clean!"

You can't imagine the force of real power (or can you?) the Master's touch spread through our entire family.

Since then we haven't been able to contain ourselves! *Lord, forgive us, your humble blabbermouths.* Jesus gave my husband his former zeal and a comeback story to tell. How could we keep quiet? We want everyone to know: The risk is worth it. Come out!

Mark 1:40–45

FOR REFLECTION: How can I allow Christ to heal something chronic in my life that now cuts me off from those I love?

A TIME TO DANCE

I speak of her in the past tense because, for all intents and purposes, our relationship died years ago.

My mother had plagued me with nagging interference until I couldn't stand another icy glare or stabbing innuendo. I avoided her, ran from her, and finally closed the lid on my life and shut her out for good.

I know it hurt her. But I couldn't muster the guts to care. Many came to her side to share her loss. To wish me back for her sake.

But I had had enough. End of case.

By and by I happened upon one who saw something in her I had never seen. Where I had seen judgmentalism and pettiness, he saw hopes and aspirations.

But sir, you don't know her like I know her.

(Imagine his seeing into your mother's heart: her dreams for you, her regrets over mistakes she'd made, her wish that she could have done a better job.)

Well, I didn't want to be disturbed.

But he had already made up his mind. He had seen enough hurt in her eyes. Perhaps he saw her as I should have seen her. *Wish I had been that kind of son.* Maybe he saw her as she had often wanted to be. (Was he seeing his own mother?) He saw a mother's joy at giving birth, the incredible urge to give life and nurture it. He saw the hours spent hoping great things for that son, the seasons given to pondering his future.

He saw my mother and felt compassion. And that's why he came up to us, stopped our dirge, and touched the relationship I had consigned to death.

I had pounded them in so firmly:

the nail of anger,
the nail of resentment,
the nail of unforgiveness.

But he pulled them out with one firm grasp: "Young man, I say to you, arise!"

I sat up. Overpowered.

He stretched out his hands toward us both: "Woman, behold your son." *Such as I am. Your son is a grand disappointment. And I'm sure to do more than one encore of failure. But maybe there's hope now. I'm game to try. Are you, Mom?*

We turned toward home. Passing through the entrance, the beams of the gate cast on my path a shadow in the shape of a cross. From behind me I heard the words of a hopeful Man: "Behold your mother."

Luke 7:11–17

FOR REFLECTION: How can Mary's Son bring new life to a relationship I've consigned to death?

THEIR KINGDOM

For the average observer, their faces would be lost in a crowd. But Jesus easily picks them out from the masses. One by one, they tell him their unrelated but similar stories:

Well, Lord, after all these years I guess I need to reintroduce myself. I was the little girl in Sunday school who eagerly recited my memory verses...the one (there must have been hundreds like me) who wanted to be a missionary.

A lot of water has passed under the bridge since those simple days when I saw everything in black and white. The complications of the real world came along, and as you know, I took up the challenges. Well, now I've got my sports car and my house overlooking the Pacific. I have more men available to me than I'm interested in.

But I'm feeling that the little girl in Sunday school somehow had a better grasp on life than I do. Is there any way to rediscover the simplicity of those days?

I take drugs to erase the pain. There's nothing to look forward to. I just want to escape it all. This is no way to live. God, if you're out there, I really need some help. I don't know where else to turn. Please.

Built a fourteen-million-dollar company in six years. Sounds pretty good, doesn't it, Lord? Self-made man, that's me. Why didn't I settle for a *one*-million-dollar company in *ten* years? No, that wouldn't have been good enough for me. Not aggressive enough. Not impressive enough. I had to cut corners, had to step on some heads.

Now I'm beached. It's not the first time. You brought me to my knees during the divorce. But I still had my pride. I could still make money better than anyone. But now I've blown even that. Jesus, I'm tired of making excuses. You've got my attention. I'm listening.

Lord, it's me again. I'm still a wreck. Since the last time we talked to each other, I've had another stupid relationship. This sap was worse than the others, if you can believe that. Took me for everything. I hate him. I hate myself worse. Yeah, I'm eating again, of course. Typical depressive me. I depress myself.

If I didn't have Carrie to live for, I don't think I would even care. I'd end it all. She's three now, you know. Cute as a bunny too.

Anyway, I'm willing to try again, Lord. I know you must be sick and tired of this. Do you have any patience left?

I must be desperate. Here I am, praying.

Basically I've climbed every mountain that challenges me, literally. Shot all the rapids I care to. Not an appealing woman in sight.

I suppose there are a few things I haven't tried, but I'm not interested enough to look for them. And going it alone has gotten old. What am I trying to prove anyway?

Why am I asking you? What do you care, right?

Dear Jesus, thank you that you love me. Thank you for dying on the cross to save me from my sins. I believe in you as my Savior.

Please come into my heart and never leave. Help me to obey my mommy. And please bring Daddy home soon. Amen.

Well, let's see. I think there's room for all of you on my lap. Everybody come in close now. That's it.

Okay, here we go. *Oouumph!*

There we are. See?

No problem.

Mark 10:13–16

FOR REFLECTION: What evidence of childlike faith shows in my life?

CHAPTER THREE

IMAGINE HIM HEARING YOUR CONCERN

Ever talked with an acquaintance for whom listening was merely a duty to endure until he could make his own point ("Well, *I* think...") or an opportunity to practice his counseling skills ("So what I hear you saying is...")?

Good listeners are not easy to come by.

I imagine that one of the greatest experiences possible would be having the Son of God listen to you with his full attention for as long as you needed it, knowing he wouldn't patronize you but would instead give you his honest response. I don't envision Jesus' eyes wandering when he listened to people. No fidgeting fingers. No impatience ("Are you finished yet?" "Hasn't that other appointment arrived, Peter?"). And I don't imagine he'd begin his reply with a pompous clearing of the throat.

In short, I surmise that he would listen to you like the true friend you need him to be. He'd hear you appropriately, neither naively nor harshly. And he'd hear you with more than his ears. He'd listen with his heart.

The way I figure it, one of the surprise blessings of heaven will be enjoying Jesus the Listener. I also figure he'd rather not wait until you get there to start.

WHERE THE BATTLE RAGES

He was a picture of dutiful conformity. His garment satisfied strict specifications. Each accessory held some meaning for those who knew how to interpret it. Even the way he groomed himself met others' expectations of him. He was a solid and secure member of a strict religious community with all the accompanying privileges and status.

And questions.

In fact, Nicodemus's mind was a battlefield. On one side were the forces of curiosity: the unexplainable healings of the sick; the confrontations with evil spirits; the amazing statements made with firm conviction ("Stop making my Father's house a house of commerce." "Destroy this temple, and in three days I will raise it up").

But his curiosity faced a looming foe: the community. The reasons to avoid the Teacher were innumerable and so convincing that they mocked even the slightest inquisitiveness. Nicodemus could hear the sting in the voices of his fellows:

"You have failed the brotherhood."

"How could you throw away all you've worked for? You have lost your rank."

"You're as good as dead."

"You have shamed your ancestors. Your family will curse you."

"The vows are sacred; break them, and you will go to your grave in shame."

"Do something foolish like that again and you will find yourself on the outside looking in."

Yet the slightest beam of light had pierced his soul. As hard as he had worked to seal all the cracks, somehow the glimmer slipped in, and now he could not deny that it intrigued him. He did not have the heart to lie to himself again.

I wonder what he would say? Would he even speak to me? If I went to talk to him, maybe he wouldn't give me a chance. Maybe he'd see what I am and deny me even a word. Well, at least I'd be free of him.

Nicodemus thought of going as someone else, of shedding the garb of his tradition and pretending he was just another religiously neutral seeker. But he didn't know how to do that. Life in the fraternity had been his food and sleep, his very life for all his life. It had been his basis of recognition and the context for all his relationships. His family life, his income, his network of essential services—everything depended on his good standing in the community.

But more than that, his very identity was inseparable from the world in which he had become entrenched. He literally could not envision himself as anything other than a Pharisee.

Why would I want to risk everything? Yet if we are right, why are we so afraid of what we know is wrong? If the Teacher is misguided, what do I have to fear from him?

His "everything to lose" seemed slightly smaller. The risk was, if just for this moment, almost worth it.

I'll have to go as I am. If he won't accept me this way, then I guess the gulf between us is meant to be.

He drew a deep breath and pulled the latch of his front door. He stepped quietly into the street. It was dark and still. He looked both ways.

Though he saw no one, he felt as if the eyes of all his brothers were burning into his chest. Nicodemus mustered the courage to take his first step, and to his delight, each step thereafter grew easier.

He chose small back alleyways for his route. (Call it instinct.) He was constantly watching, constantly feeling watched. Feeling in the wrong but driven by an inner sense that something about this journey was right.

Finally he came to the house where he had heard Jesus was staying. The crack under the door revealed a trace of light. He took confidence and knocked.

The wait for an answer seemed eternal. He was about to bolt into the darkness when the host opened the door.

"Yes?"

"Is the Teacher in?"

"This is a poor time for visitors. And besides, I doubt he needs an argument at this time of night."

"I haven't come to challenge him."

Just then a voice emerged from the living room. "Who is it, David?"

"It's a...a Pharisee."

Quickly Jesus appeared in the doorway. He stretched out a warm hand to Nicodemus. "Please come in."

And one lonely legalist stepped closer to the light.

John 2:23–3:21; 7:45–52; 19:38–42

FOR REFLECTION: Am I willing to risk being wrong to find him who is right?

THE HIGH COST OF WEALTH

The young father and businessman reclined in a soft chair on his spacious veranda, soaking in the rejuvenating sunshine. He surveyed his garden with pride and delight, for he not only observed the loveliness of the fruit trees and flowers, he also looked with joy at his young son playing and his lovely wife preparing the boy an afternoon snack.

He opened his journal to update it, pausing first to review recent entries:

MONDAY

Dissatisfaction continues to linger. I thank God for the blessings I enjoy. He has smiled on my business ventures. Yet I can't get away from the feeling that all my assets have limitations. They're temporary. Could lose them in the space of a few months.

There must be a way to add to what I've got—not just more of the same, but something different. Must be a way I can invest in something more lasting.

THURSDAY

Little Jonathan is growing up so quickly. I see a lot of myself in him. He's a bright child; he will do well in life. I see he has my strong pride though. Poor little fellow!

Heard today that Jesus is in the area. I remember hearing about him four months ago. Thought I'd like to meet him. Answer to what I'm feeling these days?

The man quickly took up his pen, eager to record the morning's events:

TUESDAY

Amazing day, though bittersweet. Got a chance to see Jesus after early meeting with my broker. Had him all to myself, one on one! Felt accepted. He seemed to appreciate my accomplishments and good conduct.

I was struck by his forthrightness. Told me what he really thought. After all the smooth talkers I've heard, it was refreshing to hear someone tell it to me straight.

Didn't tell me what I wanted to hear though. On one hand I feel he offers the solution to my problem. Would fill the void I sense. He has a certain quality about him—I can actually see him providing life on the other side.

But I never knew he demands so much. One allegiance. If he wants to succeed, he'll have to be more flexible with people, adapt to the needs of the client. I can't throw out my whole portfolio to make room for him alone. I need to be able to add to what I've already got.

Just then a three-year-old's cry of anguish interrupted his thoughts. In the yard Jonathan was trying to get to his mother, who had finished preparing jelly biscuits and grapes for him. He was trying to squeeze through a narrow opening between a tree and a fence post. By himself, the youngster could have negotiated the small passageway with ease. But he had come to treasure a tree branch he had been playing with. The branch with its leaves intact could not pass through. Unwilling to release it, Jonathan had reached a point of consternation.

His father watched the scene with a mixture of amusement and empathy. *Silly child, doesn't he know his mother's treat is so much better than that useless branch? Someday he'll learn.*

Mark 10:17–27

FOR REFLECTION: What do I cling to that keeps me from fully devoting myself to Christ?

THE FENCE

Proud she was and loyal to a fault. My mother never questioned the clan, never rebelled against the strictures placed upon us by our heritage. We were what we were, what we were created to be. Nothing could change what nature had dictated.

But for her, pride and loyalty held one flaw: They could not see her through the dark emptiness of her soul. They could not assuage the hurt. And she was too honest a person to deny the shortcomings of what everyone said should have been enough.

So she thought the unthinkable.

She looked beyond the fence for help. She dared to consider that something outside might relieve her longing.

Just as she did so, the man Jesus passed by. She was preconditioned against him: He's good but not great; he's a man for others, not for us; we were born and bred differently than he; he wouldn't care.

So they had always said.

And so she thought for the longest time, until one day she wondered if it was all true. *The signs say, "Don't cross the fence." But who wrote the signs? "He's got his own group. They're in, we're out. He doesn't listen to us." Do they know because they've tried?*

Mother had run out of hope. The world on our side of the fence didn't provide any answers. Our house was filled with devils, so filled with them that no one would even recognize one as such, much less know how to get rid of it.

We longed for relief, my mother and I. Longed for anything that would satisfy. Just one morsel of substance would be better than constant hunger pains.

When she came to me with her idea, I could see she had made up her mind (I wouldn't have stood in her way in any case). She had decided to risk it. She was going to see if Jesus would really turn her away as everyone said he would.

With every step she entertained the possibility of failure. She mounted the fence, mulling in her mind the cost of rejection by everyone she held dear. She perched herself on the post, thinking of the embarrassment she'd probably suffer when his followers spurned her. But she jumped to the ground with both feet firm in faith. *I can't go on without hope. I'll do everything I can to convince him. Even a crumb from his table would be better than starving.*

Any myths she had believed about it being miraculously easy on the other side of the fence were quickly shattered. Life on new ground felt odd and, at first, wrong. As she had feared, his followers despised her.

Crossing the border took a heavy toll. She felt like quitting. *It's just too hard. I should have observed the obvious, should have stayed where birth placed me.*

But her desperate love for her posterity drove her on. Her glimmer of hope that her children would know something better guided her through the dark storm of doubt and confusion.

Finally she found him. He confirmed her suspicion: She was not from his side of the fence.

But he heard something in her voice that told him why she had come. He sensed the length and difficulty of her journey. He saw her single-mindedness, the kind he can never turn away unrewarded.

And so he listened.

He traveled on, while Mother came home. There she found our house changed. The devils had gone.

We had made a remarkable discovery: Even crumbs of grace satisfy!

Matthew 15:21–28

FOR REFLECTION: Am I pestered by evil because I'm not single-mindedly tired of it? Do I allow preconceived—and possibly inaccurate—notions of God to keep me from his grace?

SANDSTORM!

Mention his name and from the highest court to the lowliest kitchen you would receive a knowing response. Visiting dignitaries would tell you what they'd heard of him in yonder country. Simple laborers would pass on reports from relatives who had heard him preach.

So powerful was John's ministry.

His voice carried over the unbridled expanse of the wilderness. His reputation rode, as it were, the crest of the waves of sand.

That is, until the hot winds kicked up like a blast furnace. Suddenly out of nowhere a blinding wall of darkness and confusion overcame him. It lasted for days. Tumbleweeds whirled around him, slashing his skin, taunting him for his aimlessness.

For the first time the wilderness was lonely. John needed affirmation that he was doing the right thing. Though water stood nearby, he was thirsty, needing refreshment for his soul. Was the One he preached a mirage or reality?

I have to get a message through. I have to know.

Are you the Expected One? Or have I missed it? Have I wanted so much to believe that I've fooled myself? Are those who have stayed noncommittal right after all?

All I can see right now is an endless and shapeless void, one horizon giving way to another just like it. I've lost my bearings. I need a landmark to guide me, a point to fix my eyes on.

Far away, but hardly inaccessible, Jesus stood on a hill, enjoying an unobstructed view of the valley below. He saw everything clearly. Groups of seekers came to him and, under the gently blown leaves of shade trees, received the wisdom of his teachings and the grace of his healing hands.

Jesus received John's messengers eagerly, inquiring about John's state of mind and his feelings. Welling up with compassion, Jesus empathized with his friend.

I have to get a message through. I have to let him know.

"Now that you have been here, I think you can encourage him with what you have seen:

new sight for the blind, new legs for the lame,

new strength for the diseased, new hearing for the deaf,

and new hope for the poor."

But will that assure him that I understand his concern? That I appreciate his asking about me?

"And tell him I'm grateful that he has persevered through so much. He is a blessed and faithful servant."

They traversed down the highlands to the countryside below. Crossing the lush valley carved by the river, they traveled to the deserts beyond. The highway seemed a bit smoother now, the valleys not so low, the hills not so high. And didn't the rugged places appear just a little softer than before?

They approached John's place and heard his familiar voice crying out, firmer now than they remembered it. More conviction.

As they emerged from the crowd, he nodded and grinned at them.

How did he know that we got through? And how the Master responded?

The sun was an hour yet above the horizon. The anger of the wind had calmed down as if by soothing words. The clouds of sand settled as a backdrop of pink and orange.

John went into the water and smilingly welcomed the throngs.

Let the winds blow.

Isaiah 40:3–5; Luke 7:18–28

FOR REFLECTION: Have I lost my focus on whom I serve, on the One who makes all the difference? How can I sharpen his image in my mind's eye?

CHAPTER FOUR

IMAGINE HIM TEACHING YOU

Much is said about Jesus being more than a teacher, and the point is well taken. History boasts of many great teachers, and Jesus was more than that.

But just for a moment consider how important it was that Jesus could teach and do it well. Can you imagine how different our faith would look if Jesus hadn't enjoyed teaching? If, when called upon to speak, he'd had little to say or had been bashful in front of groups surpassing a dozen in number?

Or what if people hadn't enjoyed hearing him teach? If the crowds had dwindled over time until only his relatives showed up? Or if he had been boring, and yawns had hastened him toward his conclusion?

And what if his teaching hadn't had authority? If he couldn't muster much conviction? What if his actions hadn't backed up his words?

If Jesus had not been a great teacher, the Gospels would read much differently than they do, as would the story line of your life and mine.

But not to worry. *He could teach!*

Anywhere. Anytime. Give him a mountain slope or an off-duty boat. He could teach. Put him in a stodgy synagogue, or confront him with an off-the-cuff question from a pesky opponent. He could teach.

No one's teachings are more quoted or memorized. None have so changed the course of activities on this planet.

He could teach. And after people heard him, they left saying, "We never heard anything like that before. This guy teaches with authority." Sometimes they left scratching their heads in wonder, other times babbling to their neighbors, "Can you believe that?" But they always came back for more. And you would have done the same. In fact, wouldn't it have been something:

...receiving an invitation to hear a teacher par excellence,

...going along not knowing who or what to expect,

...getting yourself situated,

...only to find out that the great teacher everyone raved about was none other than your new friend who gave you an unhurried hour of his time just the night before?

BAR MITZVAH

"That kid is going to be trouble. It's not good enough for him to recite the answers he's been taught. Where's the respect in all his questioning?"

"Look, Melchi. You, Gamaliel, and I are three old men. We've studied the sacred writings all our lives. We are answer men for thousands. What do we have to fear from a twelve-year-old boy? I say we take a more optimistic outlook. We've seen plenty of high-spirited youths in our time. They always mellow with age. Let's find out who his father is; his father's obviously a devout man. And the boy must have a very good teacher down there in Nazareth. We need to recruit this lad, with his teacher I would say, and bring them both to Jerusalem."

Melchi stood, frustration showing in the way he moved. "Cosan, you're wrong on this one. Think of the things he asked: 'Is it possible that the Servant Candle has truly been lit in our time?' 'Would you recognize Elijah if he wore skins and lived in the desert?' Come on, my friend!"

"I suppose you're right. His insistence that the Passover Lamb is yet to be eaten, not just by Israel but by the whole world, is absurd. But I still wonder if we could correct his youthful fantasies through our instruction here in the temple. We could give him the discipline he clearly lacks. What do you think, Gamaliel?"

Their friend stroked his gray beard. *What* do *I think? From my thirtieth year until now—twenty-eight years—I've been a teacher. And today I meet a lad who stretches all my boundaries. My training, the answers I've used so often to satisfy questioners...I couldn't even force the words to leave my tongue today. They rang hollow. There's something about that young man. He has me thinking in ways I've never even considered.*

"What do I think? I think we'll see more of that boy."

❧

Meanwhile, two hours outside of Jerusalem (at a caravan's pace), Joseph navigated the family cart around a pothole. He broke a long silence: "Mary, I'm baffled. I know Jesus is a special boy; I've never doubted that. But sometimes I just don't know how to handle him. With James and the other children, I know I'm fully responsible. When they do wrong, I discipline them and rarely have second thoughts. But with Jesus? It's beyond me. He stays behind in Jerusalem without telling us. You get all upset and fear that we've failed God. I'm mad, not to mention embarrassed, that I lost track of my firstborn for three whole days. Then he has the gall to ask me why I came looking for him!"

"Of course we had to look for him, Joseph."

High-pitched laughter from the back of the cart punctuated their conversation as Jesus told his two younger sisters a funny story he had heard in the city.

Mary placed her hand gently on her husband's strong forearm. "I think what he meant, honey, is that we don't have to worry about him. He's in the Father's hands."

Joseph heard the children playing. *God. His Father. He's God's Son. I'm teaching him carpentry, and he's gifted at it. But once in a while I wonder about his real work. He's learning a lot more than I'm teaching him. Where will it all lead? And where do I fit? What kind of father am I to him?*

By now Joseph's eyes were fixed on his son walking alongside the donkey and showing his younger brother how to use a long branch to make the donkey's ears twitch.

The cart creaked on.

Luke 2:39–52

FOR REFLECTION: How am I discovering the joy of being baffled by Jesus' uniqueness?

MORE THAN WORDS

It was a holiday, and I had time on my hands. I left the house to get some fresh air, told the servants I'd be back and expected to see some progress.

I noticed a crowd of people converging on the east end of town. Not knowing of any announced events, I wandered that direction out of curiosity.

As it turned out, the Nazarene was teaching. I tagged along. Soon I understood why he was so popular. "Paradoxical" is my word for him. His words didn't lead to the predictable outcomes. I liked him. (And I liked it that some people didn't.)

As the crowd grew, people began to surround me from behind, which eventually made me uncomfortable. I left, figuring I'd heard enough to think about anyway.

My steps led me down a path of questions. *What did he mean by "poor in spirit"?*

As I approached town, I saw our village "conversation piece," who often sought help from others for his livelihood. His mind not fully engaged, he couldn't support himself (or didn't care to, I often thought).

The contrast surfaced: I had accomplished a lot in my years; I had four successful sons (which boded well for my own future).

I caught myself sneering at the beggar, wondering why I was aware of my attitude today when I normally didn't recognize it. I found myself thinking about the pauper's standing in the kingdom of God; was he closer to it than I?

I continued walking and thinking. *How can I receive comfort from God?*

Presently I passed one of my rental properties. Because of late payments, I had served an eviction notice to the family staying there. The children saw me approaching and ran to their mother, hiding behind her skirt.

Maybe I don't need as much rent from that unit as I'm charging. They could probably manage to stay in the house if I lowered the rate.

I walked by, offering a smile and a wave for a change. The burden of my own financial woes seemed a bit lighter.

Before long I encountered some young boys fighting.

Blessed are peacemakers.

Turns out it was a small misunderstanding. Why I got involved I don't know. Guess it struck me that boys are people too.

When I walked into my house, I remembered that my wife and I had not parted company on good terms.

But wives are people too.

I asked her if we could share a hot drink together and talk. As I waited for her to bring the cups, I contemplated the words I had heard on the mountain. But even more than that, I reflected on the spirit of the man who spoke those words. It was contagious. I wanted to be like him. Wanted to treat beggars and renters and my wife the way he would.

I chuckled inwardly. *Are people changing, or is it me?*

The tea arrived. It was more bitter than I like, but I drank it anyway. The conversation was sweet enough to compensate.

Matthew 4:23–5:12

FOR REFLECTION: What chances am I giving Christ's words to get off the page and into my heart, where they belong?

MARY'S SONG

The oil lamp flickered well into the night. Martha and Lazarus were asleep, and the house was quiet as Mary took up her stylus and poured out her thoughts to the Lord. What flowed onto the page was a conversation that set her free....

O Lord, it greatly heartens me to think upon your words,
for you told me you enjoyed my presence more than noble works.
But I must tell you honestly, I find it very hard
to know I've really chosen what you call "the better part."
I envy the accomplishments, the good that others do;
I don't have much to offer to prove my love for you.
The looks I get from others, my feeling of fatigue—
could it be I'm not the person you think you see in me?

Child, I tell you now in stillness what I said among the din—
the only thing I look for is a longing heart within.
I'm not looking for performance. I don't care if you're the best.
I desire your companionship. I want to give you rest.

That you could want my company, though I struggle so,
is a greater gift of comfort than you could ever know.
O Savior, take my sadness, my ever-wand'ring heart,
and forever reassure me that it is the better part.

The turmoil of your inner life will rarely settle down;
chaos and confusion will always come around.

But you can learn to rest while striving, sit while standing tall.
I promise I'll be listening, no matter when you call.
So come aside and learn of me; there's room here at my feet.
Your tender heart's desire is the only thing I need.
I tell you now in stillness what I said among the din—
the only thing I look for is a longing heart within.

Luke 10:38–42

FOR REFLECTION: Do I give myself permission to receive Christ's compliments even though I still struggle in my walk with him?

DEATH BY FAMILIARITY

"Today this scripture is fulfilled in your hearing."
"Isn't this Joseph's son?"

Like a full lunar eclipse to one who refuses to look skyward,
Like the eyes that view creation and see only happenstance,
Is the one who takes offense and misses an encounter with greatness.

So, he's back.

Is that supposed to thrill me? Am I supposed to give him the keys to our city as well?

Sorry, I'm fresh out of red carpets.

Why can't Joseph's son be content to stay where he belongs? What's wrong with honoring his father and being a faithful citizen? ("We could even make him an official of the synagogue.") There are some nice available girls here. ("He is even more handsome than before he left.") He could settle down here and raise sons. He builds a pretty good cabinet. Why doesn't he take his rightful place in the family trade?

[Joseph's son unrolls the scroll.]

("How well he reads." "Mary must be so proud.")

I'm not just some poor man, destitute of hope. I've known Joseph's son since he climbed trees in our streets. Who is he to talk of good news, as if I should take it from him as a handout like anyone else from Capernaum?

Fancy him talking as if I were a prisoner, confined behind bars. Do I look like I'm a captive? He's just one of us; imagine him talking about release.

He never bothered with our blind before. Why did he have to go to

Galilee first and see to the needs of their blind? What does our carpenter's son know about sight?

We have our share of battered and abused. Oppression is no stranger in our houses. But we won't be likened to just any old town along this ridge.

[The scroll, open but for a moment, is closed.]

Joseph's son went away and became famous. Then he comes back to us and expects us to set everything aside and make a big deal over him. He should have thought things through before he went out and put Cana on the map. Should have planned a bit better before trying to get support from us. He'll have to learn that if he wants us to dance to his music, he'll have to play our tune.

After all, we knew him before others did. Taught his classes and bought his wares long before others even knew his name. Now he comes back with not even a word of appreciation. No recognition that we go back farther than most.

We know Joseph's son all too well. We're too familiar with him to get that excited.

[The attendant puts the scroll back on its stand, in its familiar place. He covers it, as if to protect it from any further risk.]

Too bad he lost touch with the people who knew him when he was nothing. I mean, after all, what is Joseph's son doing, talking like he's God's Son and Joseph's God?

Luke 4:16–30

FOR REFLECTION: Do I take Jesus for granted?

CHAPTER FIVE

IMAGINE HIM TELLING YOU STORIES

The parables of Jesus sort out humanity: They draw or they repel. Those on the way to Christ find in his stories reasons to keep coming. Those deciding they don't need him find in his parables more evidence to go it alone.

Why do Jesus' stories divide people into these two camps? It's not because they're so difficult or mysterious that only superb minds can figure them out. Nor is it because their meaning is found only by those holding special information. The meaning of the parables is available to anyone.

The key is in the wanting to. The needing to.

The heart of a king or a child can be drawn to Jesus instead of repelled. Faith is the only requirement.

Which is why so many people during Jesus' day found in his stories reasons to reject him: Their hearts were dull (Matthew 13:10–17).

If you were in a crowd listening to Jesus and his eyes met yours, what would he see in you? Growing distance or a look saying, "Tell me more"?

His parables are still sorting people out. So make sure you hear them. Be sure your eyes invite him in. Come and look afresh at Jesus the storyteller.

Day after day he had seen it in its case,
gazing on its pristine beauty.
Until one day he freed it from its place
to view it in the sunlight clearly.
And when he did, the beam pierced through;
with eyes awakened did he see.
O friend, do take a look anew
for that same jeweler you can be.

THE GOOD SAMARITAN

Philip was deeply appreciative for what he had heard. "That was an inspiring story, Lord. I'm really going to be more caring from now on."

"Good, Philip. I'll look forward to seeing the fruit of your sympathetic heart. Be aware, though, that sometimes there's more to the story."

"More to the story?"

"Let me tell it to you this way. Once, as a man was traveling, he fell among thieves. He was beaten up, robbed, and left for dead along the side of the road. Later, two other travelers passed by. One was a priest, the other a Levite. Both saw the injured man but decided not to get involved, passing by on the other side.

"Meanwhile, a Samaritan started out on a journey of his own, intending to travel along the same road as the priest and Levite. But the Samaritan had some difficulties before he even set off. His donkey stumbled in the courtyard and came up limping. But as he had only the one donkey, the Samaritan had to use it anyway.

"After he finally got going, the Samaritan passed by the marketplace. There he met a group of beggars who almost always accosted him when he went that way. He never knew whether to help them. He felt compassion for them in their poverty, but he wondered if giving them money actually helped keep them in a lifestyle of begging. ('Why get a job when we can make more money begging alms?') But when he considered withholding his surplus to encourage them to make an honest living, he often felt guilty of stinginess.

"He decided on this particular day to err on the side of generosity, so he gave a coin to one of the beggars, telling him to buy only bread with it and to share it with the others. (He knew they often used alms for their habit of drunkenness, but by now the shops were closed, and the Samaritan couldn't buy them bread himself.)

"As he resumed his journey, the Samaritan thanked God that he did not have to live a life dependent on others. Soon he passed out of the city gates. He dreaded this experience because, being a Samaritan, he would often have to undergo the overly ambitious interrogation of the city officials. Sure enough, they pulled him aside and gave him trouble. On this particular day they found something they did not like about the load he had packed on his donkey. What was he carrying, and where was he going? Before long they got to their real point: a bribe. Couldn't he come up with a little something for the pocket? Just something small, they said.

"The Samaritan launched into his usual response: 'I am not the kind of man to give a bribe. Yes, of course it's not a bribe you want, just a little something to grease the wheels of commerce. But still, I don't do that. In fact, I will stand here till the sun goes down, and I will not give you anything. Yes, I would even go to prison for the principle of it. I am certainly sorry for appearing suspicious. Next time I'll try to avoid giving that impression...'

"They finally let him leave the city after indicating that they were releasing him only because of their great tolerance.

"By this time the Samaritan's attitude was very strained. He wondered if he should even attempt the rest of the trip, given the bad mood he was in. Just as he was muttering his dissatisfaction to himself, he came upon the unfortunate man who had been mugged and left alongside the road.

"'What bad luck,' he thought to himself. 'Why did it have to be *me* who happened along this trail at this time? *Anyone* seeing this poor victim would surely have helped out. Why couldn't it have been someone who was having an otherwise good journey?'

"He stood over the man, pondering his options. He looked to the left and to the right.

"The poor man, half delirious, spoke from the ground. The slur of his speech indicated he was nearly drunk. 'Help me, sir, 'cause if you don't, I'll claim *you* did this to me.'

"The Samaritan was incredulous! What a callous remark from a helpless man. (Actually a thought of thankfulness shot through his mind that the 'victim' was not a trap, cooperating with accomplices waiting to attack from the bushes.)

"His compassionate side won out. He loaded the man on his already struggling beast. By the grace of God, they made it to an inn with the donkey limping all the way. (The animal would probably have to be put down after the trip.)

"The Samaritan told the innkeeper to give the man whatever care he needed. As the words left his mouth, he wondered if he was making a mistake. What guarantee did he have that the manager would bill him honestly or give the victim proper care?

"As he left the hotel, the Samaritan debated whether to say something to testify of his faith or to remain quiet and not appear overly pious. Passing under the doorway, he managed a lukewarm, 'May the Lord bless you.' He mounted the donkey, grabbed the reins, and with a jerk vented a little frustration, coaxing his reluctant beast into its first ginger steps. He found his way back to the trail with mixed feelings about his journey.

"You see what I mean, Philip? As you live the life of a good Samaritan, be ready for the occasional bad day."

Luke 10:25–37

FOR REFLECTION: Would I rather live an uncluttered life because I rarely help others, or would I rather be someone who, already somewhat frazzled, decides to help yet again?

SPURIOUS ILLUSIONS IN THE PEWS

Envision Jesus telling this parable to certain ones who trusted their own righteousness and viewed others with contempt:

"There were four men among those who attended a community Thanksgiving service. Various churches of different denominations participated. Several pastors preached during the annual event, a sign of unity among the churches in the town. Near the end of the meeting, there was a time for silent prayer.

"The man from Fifth Fundamental prayed silently this way: 'God, I thank thee that I am not like other people, such as this lady in front of me, who have no more basis for their faith than their flimsy experiences, which they manufacture to say they are blessed by you. And thank you that I'm more mature than that lawyer across the aisle—must be from Liberal United. I saw him having a glass of wine with a client over at Firkin and Steak last month. I've never had a drop, and if I may say so, Lord, I'm proud of it. Thank you that I haven't missed my tithes and offerings for—how many years is it now?—yes, seventeen and three-quarter years. And thank you, God, for helping me raise my kids in your ways, never allowing them to attend a movie or go with friends to any parties. Speaking of the kids, help Jeanne and Chris forsake their rebellion and walk the "straight and narrow" again, Lord.'

"The man from Holiness on High prayed this way: 'O Lord, praise your holy name! Thank you that you delivered me out of Pastor Blight's church. Thank you that I'm no longer resisting your will for Christians! These poor people around here. Look at them. They're all dead. Like that fundamentalist fellow over there—an "Alleluia" or two would do him a world of good, but it would probably crack his cheeks to smile. Or that lawyer—probably doesn't even know you as Savior and Lord. I'm sure he doesn't have the baptism. Pastor Bill was the only one up there tonight who had the Spirit. (Help his sons to come back to you, Lord.) Thank you that I attend a church where the pastor has the gift of healing. And I'm so glad I prevailed until I got the gift of tongues.'

"The man from Liberal United prayed, 'God, I thank you that I'm not like so many of these fanatics in here, like that narrow-minded Bible-thumper across the aisle. How many church splits has he caused, I wonder? And what's-his-name over there from—what is that place called?—Halos on High? Thank you for keeping all those demon chasers together in one place where they can't harm the general public. Those types wouldn't know a social cause if it came up and bit 'em on the a— ('scuse my French, Lord). I head our commission on AIDS Awareness, and I raised over ten thousand dollars in pledges for our program to the indigent last year. Nothing to sneeze at, eh, Lord?'

"The fourth man had slipped in during the middle of the service. He sat near the back door off to the side. Some of the churchgoers in town joked about him, saying that the way he wandered from church to church was at least consistent with his name: Mr. Pilgrim. He often felt discouraged and had probably received free counseling from half the clergymen on the platform.

"Pilgrim, deliberately sitting off by himself, couldn't even lift his eyes to look around. Twisting his frumpy cap in his hands, he prayed simply, 'God, be merciful to me, a sinner!'

"I tell you, this man, rather than the others, went to his house justified. For everyone who exalts himself shall be humbled, but he who humbles himself shall be exalted."

Luke 18:9–14

FOR REFLECTION: Have my circle of friends and I become so convinced of our righteousness that we've lost our openness to true humility?

PARABLE OF THE SOILS

One morning four neighbors walked out of their houses only to find that during the night a nicely decorated package had been left by the door of each house.

The packages were identical, even down to the notes affixed to the outside. Each simply read: "This is a gift to the resident of this house. You may do with it what you will. The giver will return in one month from tonight if you would care to meet him."

When the month had elapsed, the gift giver revisited each home. He arrived quite late, and all the residents had gone to sleep. But before doing so, each one had left something on the front step in case the gift giver came during the night.

At the first house, the gift giver found only a note. It read: "Dear sir, I thank you kindly for the gift you left me. Unfortunately the very day I received it, I had to rush off to work. When I returned home, I found that someone had broken into my house and stolen the package. I thought at first that I had simply misplaced it, but having searched the house, I'm convinced it was taken. So sorry."

The second house held a different response. The package was laid by the door exactly where the gift giver had placed it a month earlier. It was unopened. Attached was this message: "Thank you! Thank you! How lovely of you to leave a gift for me. I was simply overjoyed to receive it. The wrapping paper is the most exquisite I have ever seen. I savored the present for days, waiting for just the right time to open it. I finally decided to do so when my relatives were over for a visit. But as I explained the circumstances of my receiving it, they expressed grave concern about the wisdom of opening it at all. They thought it ill-advised to accept a gift from someone whose identity I didn't even know. So I return it to you with thanks and regret. Again, thank you, but please understand."

Withdrawing the package, the gift giver proceeded to the next house where he found the gift lying in its place, unwrapped. It, like the others, was a book, and on its flyleaf was a note saying, "To the giver of this gift. This is a splendid book on building model ships. I thank you kindly for presenting it to me. When I first opened it, I thought to myself this was just the hobby I had searched for. In fact, I wondered if I might build models to give as presents to my friends. I've come to realize, however, that I haven't got the time for such a pursuit. I'm afraid I just have too many other things I'm responsible for. Please accept it back, with the hope you will find another who will have some use for it."

Disappointed, yet seemingly unsurprised, the gift giver moved on to the final house. What he saw delighted him. He was relieved to find the step was not empty, yet it did not hold the book either. Instead, he saw one carefully built model ship, complete with sails.

He reached into his pocket and extracted a small piece of cloth. Reaching down, he placed it as a flag on the tallest mast. It read: "Well done."

Mark 4:1–20

FOR REFLECTION: What evidence proves that God's Word has taken root in my heart?

DEBTORS PRISON

Is your hurt deep? Have you felt it repeatedly? Find yourself ensnared in a cycle of unforgiveness?

Imagine Jesus telling it this way:

"A certain king wanted to settle accounts with all his servants. One servant brought before him owed a surprisingly large sum. The servant must have been employed by the king for many years to have amassed a debt larger than twenty years' worth of income.

"Since the servant owed so much and had no means with which to pay the debt, the king made the right and just decision: The servant would need to sell everything he possessed—including selling his family into slavery—to repay what he owed.

"The servant begged for mercy. He promised to repay. He fell down on his knees before the king.

"The king knew the helplessness of the servant's plight, and so he considered forgiving the debt completely. As he pondered what he should do, the king investigated the servant's history. He found there was more to the servant's story than was obvious. The king discovered, for instance, that the servant had been chronically negligent in repaying many loans; this led the king to believe the servant was undisciplined and lacked appreciation for the privilege of borrowing. The king also considered that forgiving the loan might communicate weakness on his part. It could lead to others trying to take advantage of his graciousness.

"And so, for several good reasons forgiveness did not make sense. In fact, logic opposed the idea.

"But the king chose to forgive the entire debt anyway.

"The king expected that freedom from the heavy burden would

transform the servant's outlook. The king could envision the servant going out and dispensing grace and forgiveness generously.

"But the servant did not react that way. Instead, he went and found a fellow servant who owed him a small amount. The debt was so paltry it likely had been incurred only recently or had been unconsciously forgotten by the debtor. Nevertheless, the first servant attempted to collect his money with a vengeance more appropriate to a large debt or a vicious offense. Anger had distorted his perspective. He demanded immediate repayment or else.

"The servant who owed fell down on his knees. He begged for mercy. He promised to repay.

"The other servant, the one with the power, realized the helplessness of his debtor, so he considered forgiving the debt completely.

"But he chose not to. Instead, he threw the powerless servant into prison.

"When the king heard about it, he was very angry. In fact, extremely angry. The king called for the first servant to come and explain his action.

"The king said, 'How could you be so wicked? I forgave you a massive debt you could not possibly have repaid. Could you not have extended mercy to one who owed you comparatively little?'

"The servant replied, 'It may seem little to you, my lord, but I cannot see the debt as small. And there's more to the story than you may realize. This slave has been chronically negligent repaying me and others. It's time someone taught him a lesson.

"'Not only that, sire, I owed him a debt once, and he wouldn't forgive me. Normally I wouldn't worry about such a small debt, but I can't let him think he can take advantage of me. Forgiving him would have communicated weakness on my part.

"'And consider this as well: This other servant is basically undisciplined and probably would not appreciate what a favor I did in loaning him money in the first place. So you can see why I had every reason not to forgive. And that's why I have sent him to prison—right where he belongs.'

"'I see exactly what you mean,' answered the king. (The servant smiled contentedly.)

"'...which is why I know you could have chosen to forgive anyway.' (Consternation crept over the servant's face as he began to recognize his new surroundings.)

"'When you chose to withhold grace from another, you forfeited grace yourself. Your choice not to forgive was itself a verdict.'

"The servant glanced around. He found himself in a cell.

"Little did he know that he had been the judge.

"Little did he know that he still held the key."

Matthew 18:21–35

FOR REFLECTION: Has my unwillingness to forgive robbed me of the joy of being truly forgiven?

CHAPTER SIX

IMAGINE HIM SHOWING YOU HIS POWER

There is a Greek word for strength that even sounds strong: *pantokrator.*

It consists of two words that pack a punch in their own right: *pantos,* meaning "all," and *kratos,* meaning "might." Together they form a powerful concept: "Almighty."

But it's more than a concept. It's a name. A person.

Watch for it at the end of Revelation 1:8: "'I am the Alpha and the Omega,' says the Lord God, 'who is, and who was, and who is to come, the Almighty.'"

Pantokrator, the almighty Jesus Christ.

He who has never been nonexistent.

He who commands the armies of heaven with a word.

He who created all the macroworlds, where planets form galaxies and galaxies form the universe.

He who created all the microworlds, where ants build their intricate subterranean palaces and where neutrons and protons shake hands unfailingly in bilateral agreement.

Consider.

What would it be like if the Pantokrator visited his creation? If he visited those made of the weak elements of the earth? Those who would be blinded by the light of his heavenly glory and blown apart by the sheer force of his raw power?

Could we survive a visit from the Lord of heaven? Absolutely not!

It would kill us. We would be shrapnel, detonated by the immeasurable power of his purity and his brilliance.

Not to mention his judgment. Simply being exposed to the complete holiness of his character would make us so aware of our own uncleanness that guilt and shame would implode us in an instant.

Could we survive a visit from him whose name is above every other name, both now and in the phenomenal age to come? Certainly not!

Then why did we? Why did we survive his coming?

Because of the most incredible miracle of self-restraint eternity has ever witnessed. For our own protection, he gave us only the slightest peek at his power.

But oh, what a peek!

And how suitable.

Not enough to destroy us. But more than enough to change us.

OBJECT OF WRATH, OBJECT OF MERCY

"As for you, you were dead in your transgressions and sins,
in which you used to live
when you followed the ways of this world
and of the ruler of the kingdom of the air,
the spirit who is now at work in those who are disobedient.
All
of
us
also lived among them at one time,
gratifying the cravings of our sinful nature
and following its desires and thoughts.
Like the rest, we were
by
nature
objects of wrath."
EPHESIANS 2:1–3

Imagine being so completely entrenched in territory dominated by evil that you cannot envision anyone ever reaching you from the outside.

Imagine the shame you'd feel at your behavior. Your awareness of others' opinions about your disgusting life is compounded by your total inability to change, to take control of your life again. The person you once were can never be again.

The torment is continual. Never do you have the relief of a good night's sleep. Never do the voices stop their condemnations and accusations. Never does the fear or the filth subside.

Always the living death.

Others have tried to control you. Well-meaning practitioners have sought to protect you (or protect others from you) by confining you or isolating you.

But the forces inside have become overpowering. Finally you reach complete self-hatred. If life is a gift, you want to return it. You despise all you are.

Imagine the mixture of emotions in seeing the Son of God approach your turf.

On the one hand, the voices within begin to clamor and curse:

"Who the—does he think he is, coming into our area?"

"—, kill the—!"

The demons are tormented by the invasion of holiness. Nothing can wreak greater havoc on an evil settlement than a quiet appearance by the Son of Righteousness.

So familiar are the loud voices that they seem your own. You hate the one they hate. You try to deceive the one they fear: "What do you want with me, Jesus, Son of the Most High God? Swear to God you won't torture me!"

At the same time, in the midst of all the shouting and turmoil within, a still voice whispers. You hear it so seldom anymore, yet it has been with you for a long time, perhaps the longest. It's childlike. Innocent. Honest.

It's your voice: "Could there still be hope?"

Imagine the strong force that has long dominated you suddenly begging for mercy. Suddenly disarmed in the presence of real power. Suddenly negotiating for some semblance of dignity in defeat.

Only in the feeling of freedom do you realize how truly captive you have been. Only in the cutting of the cords do you understand why you have been so helpless to deliver yourself.

But when the burden is removed from your back, you know you'll never need to return to slavery again.

In place of the cacophony, there's quiet. For the first time in memory, you can follow a thought from the trailhead to the summit, undisturbed and unassaulted. The relief is indescribable.

Imagine your life suddenly meaning something. That which you had surrendered is now your permanent possession. No longer a disgrace. Now hopeful.

"Go home to your family and tell them how much the Lord has done for you and how he has had mercy on you."

You mean you're giving me responsibility? You have a job you want me to do? Lord, a thousand demons could not keep me from serving you now! I'll tell my family all right. I'll speak the truth till I die.

Imagine having such a story to tell and telling it without losing your train of thought.

Mark 5:1–20

"But because of his great love for us,
God, who is
rich
in
mercy,
made us alive with Christ
even when we were dead in transgressions—it is by grace
you have been saved."
EPHESIANS 2:4–5

FOR REFLECTION: Am I aware of the deliverance (whether traumatic and sudden, or gradual and quiet) that Jesus has brought about in my life?

FROM ANGER TO WONDER

Frankly I had trouble seeing any point in taking a new direction. I was perfectly content to stay where I was.

The Lord is obviously no novice at this kind of journey. He ought to have known that you can always count on turbulence in these situations.

So why did he have us launch out? *This is stupid, Lord.*

Now the winds slap us around like a punch-drunk sailor on his first shore leave. The gale mocks our courage…or stupidity. I think we may go down. Anger washes over me. *How insensitive of him! Irresponsible. I'm going to die because of a whim of God!* (What could be worse than the Master sending you in a certain direction and then falling asleep?)

"Lord, I need you! I'm about to go under! Don't you care? Are you even listening? Are you going to sleep through this whole storm? I'm going under!"

(I think of it now with chagrin. Imagine the absurdity of being angry with the Son of God for allowing me to encounter life's inevitable trouble! As if being in his company somehow entitled me to less turmoil than the next boatload of pilgrims.)

Before we capsize, he wakes up. I don't know how long before. It seems he wakes only a moment before we would surely go down. But how urgent is it really? He seems to know.

Jesus stands. Effortlessly balancing himself on the bow of our lurching vessel, he speaks as a mother to a fussing infant, "Shhh, be still now."

The voice itself is enough to calm, never mind the authority.

All is placid.

Safe.

Imagine how small I feel when he turns and looks directly into my eyes.

Am I the only one who panicked? Why does his gaze always land on me?

"Why are you so timid? How is it that you have no faith?"

No faith? I have faith. I've soaked in your teaching all day. You're the greatest. But who can think of faith at a time like this?

It dawns on me that he doesn't intend to rebuke me. No, he wants to lovingly disciple me. Such a bizarre life I've found myself in. Following him makes each day an adventure. I realize I love this man. I'd do anything for him. Somehow he never fails to come through. Not always as I expect or when. But he does. Even when the wind and sea stand in his way!

Why do you despair, O my soul? And why are you continually disturbed within me? Shhh. Be still now.

Mark 4:35–41

FOR REFLECTION: Am I angry at God for the turbulence he allows in my life and for what seems like his inattention to my plight?

WHEN POWER IS PERFECTED

In retrospect, it had been God's sovereign timing that wove three paths into one.

Along one of the paths came a child. (Do you know him?) He had faced special challenges from earliest childhood, struggled to make it. He often spent his days in confusion, swirling like the wind in self-destruction. It seemed that just when he felt he could express his anguish, the ability would leave him. His behavior set him apart from the crowd. Was it the ridicule or the pity that was worse?

The boy's lot in life created a strain on all around him: parents, siblings, extended family. They wanted to love him, and they did. But it was difficult living with an embarrassment, difficult to know whether to fight those who made fun or to agree with them.

The stress of his special needs made others short on patience. Not wanting to take it out on the child, the family too often became a battleground as one turned his frustrations on another. It was a family barely coping with a special calling.

Along the second path came the parent. (You likely know him, too.) The trail he had walked was marked by desperate attempts to find help for his son. He had made expensive visits to people touting special abilities at diagnosis and treatment. He had spared no expense in hopes he could unearth the secret to his son's healing. But help had proven a mirage. In fact, the boy's condition had worsened with time. Practitioners' boasts had no substance. Charlatans they were, and the "friends" who had recommended them were accomplices.

Not surprisingly, the parent had turned cynical, finding little reason to believe that anyone could help his child, that he should make even one more effort.

Why then did he reach out to Jesus? Was it brokenheartedness for his suffering one that drove him? Or anger at the embarrassment and shame?

Up the third path traveled Jesus' followers, people like you and me. People of faith, convinced that Jesus was the answer to fractured relationships, weakened bodies, and troubled minds.

Yet their journey had revealed their ineptness. They had tried to help the suffering child, had responded in love to a father's desperate cries. But they had failed. (Can you identify with them?)

So now they felt overwhelmed by the task before them. Living for Jesus and representing him had not proved to be easy. ("What if the boy had died?")

They traveled three paths of weakness that converged at the Source of strength. Jesus met them there: The child found healing, the parent comfort, the disciples challenge.

And then he turned toward the mountain and walked straight at it. "We'll never be able to cross over that mountain," they said. "It's too high."

"No, it's not too high."

The father took hold of his child's hand. The disciples followed in turn. From the paths they had walked, they brought their unanswered questions, their humility, and their faith, which seemed inadequate for the tasks that lay ahead of them.

They did not know where the path would lead, but they each felt convinced that it was the right route to take. *We believe. Help our unbelief.*

Mark 9:14–29; Matthew 17:14–20

FOR REFLECTION: Is faith still a chore, or is it becoming a rest?

BRIMMING WITH THE BEST

As always, events were unfolding on two levels: the Obvious and the Significant. By the end of the day, Mary would be aware of them both.

It happened at a wedding celebration in Cana, a neighboring town of Nazareth. I surmise that the bride or groom was related to Mary. In the Eastern culture, a wedding (like a funeral) is one of the biggest family events of the year. The bride and groom invite anyone remotely related to them, and friends of friends cannot be turned away.

Apparently many shirttail relatives arrived at this particular wedding. Hence the problem: depleted wine.

You know the story. And you know the feelings—the sense of responsibility, a feeling of helplessness—and it all happened in public view.

Life on the level of the Obvious.

Mary turned toward Jesus, brought her hand nonchalantly up to her mouth, and moved her lips as little as possible. "So many people have come we've run out of wine."

I know you can do something. Thirty years raising you have taught me that.

Then came the reply she didn't want to hear: "Relax, this isn't your party; it's not your problem. And it's not my time yet."

(Here we can pull back the curtain just a bit for a glimpse of the Significant: Heaven is on tiptoe. The breath of the angels is trapped in their glorified lungs. And the Father cracks a smile because he knows what's coming but is keeping it to himself. You see, all creation waits for the revealing of the Son of God. The good wine is bursting at the seams to get out!)

"It's not time." The words reverberated on heaven and earth.

But the Spirit has *come upon me.*

"It's not time."

Though I have *endured the Temptation.*

"It's not time."

The Father has *given me permission.*

"It's not time."

But this is *my mother.*

"Fill the water pots!"

(At this point in his-story, there is a major gap in kingdom progress. Heavenly quiet is shattered, giving way to uncontrolled backslapping and rip-snorting, celebrative pandemonium, all under the blessing of the Father's perfect joy.)

Back to the Obvious. Several things are happening now.

The headwaiter has never worked such a party. He has never tasted such quality wine, and where did the groom get 120 gallons of the stuff?

Speaking of the groom, he's grinning from ear to ear. He winks at his bride as if to say, "Stick with me, kid."

There are the servants, who saw what happened. Or did they? (They must have discussed that wedding for months afterward. Their only relief probably came after the more skeptical servants talked the rest of them out of believing the miraculous.)

And then there was Mary. Responsible Mary. Stressed Mary. Hopeful but submissive Mary. ("Whatever he says to you, do it.")

Now she's the mother made proud by her son. He didn't just make enough. He made plenty. Not just passable but the best. *Why did I worry? Why did I whisper? Now I wish I had shouted to him across the room!*

I'm guessing, but maybe after all the guests were gone and the dishes were washed and put away, when the floor was swept and a breeze had cooled the room again, maybe Mary found a soft chair off in a corner, poured herself a cup of the good burgundy everyone had raved about, propped her tired legs on a stool, and chuckled just a bit as she took her first sip.

She had seen the Significant.

Old wineskins, brace yourselves. The party's just beginning.

"Mmm, that *is* good."

John 2:1–11

FOR REFLECTION: In stressful situations where does the pressure come from? Why do I worry? (Find a soft chair.)

PART TWO

IN THE DAYTIME PATHS OF DEEPER COMPANIONSHIP

The opening chapters of your relationship with Christ are essential. "Rereading" them, as we have been doing together, invigorates the soul.

But they don't represent the full story. There's more.

Christ doesn't expect your relationship with him to remain in the getting-acquainted stage. In fact, something's wrong if you see Jesus only as a teacher you respect or a miracle worker you admire.

With some people you find that after you've become well acquainted, you can only go so far. Only so much of the person's qualities or goals interest you, or your friend has blocked you from going deeper and discovering more.

You won't find your friend Jesus that way on either count. He wants you to know him more deeply. He wants to walk with you for long periods of time so you can see more of his substance...and so he can know you better.

He wants to include you in his discipleship training. Look at how he took the Twelve to a level of friendship that the larger crowds never enjoyed. When he came to a thorny situation that required strict measures or a difficult reply, Jesus didn't dismiss the disciples, asking them to return at a "more opportune time." Instead, he took them along; he included them. They saw most of what he saw. They heard most of what he said, publicly and privately. As a result, the pathways of companionship revealed Jesus' anger and his tears. They heard his rebukes and his laughter.

But as healthy relationships deepen, both parties feel the impact. In other words, Jesus doesn't intend to be the only one sharing and opening up. He expects you to reciprocate.

So the growth of your friendship with Christ brings the discovery that you're in a relationship meant to stretch you and change you. He challenges you to be as transparent with him as he is with you, to let your weaknesses show so that you may grow.

That's why Jesus challenges you to go beyond your limits.

Again, his pattern with the disciples bears this out. He called them to leave their nets. He beckoned Peter out onto the waves. He pushed the boundaries of their faith: "You *feed the thousands."*

The challenge of these pathways stretches us to grow in at least two key areas.

One is trust. Higher terrain causes us to ask: Can I trust Jesus to continue to value my friendship even after he knows my faults? (And how will he react when he discovers them? With anger? Disappointment? Under-standing? Correction?) Will I prove worthy of his trust in me as he lets me know more about him (especially if I find certain aspects of his life or certain ways he does things surprising or difficult to accept)?

Then there's the challenging territory of expectations: Now that we've established the existence of our relationship, what should we expect of each other? What is fair for Jesus to ask of me? (And what will I do if I think he asks too much? Or is that even possible, since he is God in addition to being my friend?) Do I have the right to expect anything from him? (How insistent can I be? Are we just "playing friendship," or is there real give-and-take where I have a right to certain expectations?)

By now it hardly needs saying: The way to deeper companionship is not always straight and smooth. It's harder to navigate than the blossoming fields of first discovery.

In fact, at times when walking more closely with Christ, a part of you will want to turn back and enjoy a less involved acquaintance. Less conflict and fewer challenges can be appealing. Walking the trails is tiring. And some, not surprisingly, have chosen to go back. Such was the decision of a few who had become acquainted with him. They liked what they heard, but after discovering some of Christ's more difficult teachings, they stopped following him (John 6:60, 66).

But others—and I trust you and I are joining them—took up the challenge of the winding and sometimes treacherous path of true relationship. In response to the other desertions, Jesus asked the Twelve if they wanted to resign as well. Can we not echo Peter's reply? "Lord, to whom shall we go? You have the words of eternal life. We believe and know that you are the Holy One of God" (John 6:68–69).

We willingly take up the walk with Christ when we realize that he is Truth Incarnate, that somehow he is all that ultimately matters, that even if we let everything else fall away, we absolutely must cling with all our might to him.

Africa, where I live, teaches a lot about paths. Nothing profound, but helpful in this context. First, paths take time to walk. You don't quickly reach the end. Second, completing a path usually requires many little steps. But the steps add up, and in time you find, looking back, that you've made fairly significant progress. And third, if you stop before a path ends, there's a good chance you're in the middle of nowhere.

In Africa, even a child knows these truths.

Think about that, and keep going.

CHAPTER SEVEN

IMAGINE HIM WALKING WITH YOU

Jesus must have made good use of the transportation systems of his day. As he assisted his father, Joseph, in the carpentry business, Jesus would have, at times, manned the reins of a cart or wagon to transport a load of timber or deliver a piece of handmade furniture. And Jesus probably rode mules when available; we know that on one special occasion he rode a colt into Jerusalem.

But for the most part, Jesus got around by walking dirt trails and narrow alleyways just like the vast majority of his contemporaries, just like most of the world's population today.

Four men—Matthew and Mark, Luke and John—have given us their written accounts of Jesus' public ministry. Next time you read their chronicles, pay special attention to a twofold theme: (1) how much Jesus walked and (2) how often others wanted to walk with him.

(Well, wouldn't you?)

You might also want to note how often Jesus asked others to walk with him. He enjoyed companions. And as he walked with them, he imparted to them his life and teachings. (Surely there's a lesson here for would-be disciple makers.)

Whenever you slip vicariously into the sandals of those who had the privilege of literally walking with Jesus, remember that through the wonder of his Spirit who indwells the believing heart, you can walk with him, too.

Today.

And as you do, keep your eyes and ears open. Because when you walk with Jesus, it's only a matter of time before something wild happens!

HE'S NOT FUSSING!

Chest-high in a breeze-blown sea of soft grain. My best friends fore and aft. Walking. Joking. Listening. Snacking.

Our leader and friend right here among us. Sharing. Clarifying. Laughing.

Never been happier. A man with good friends, intoxicated with wholesome joy.

Wish I could feel this way forever. Is it okay to have this much fun?

"Hey, you can't do that!"

Knew it was coming.

"Don't you fools know the rules?"

Yeah, we know the rules, but somehow they didn't seem very important.

"The rules have been around for a long time. You've got to stick to them. Don't just go off enjoying yourself any time you want!"

But aren't the rules from God? Didn't he write them? Or did he?

Couldn't God "upgrade" the rules if he chose to? I mean, Jesus doesn't seem particularly worried about breaking any rules. Why fuss when even Jesus isn't fussing?

With soft-spoken firmness, our leader queries the critics: "Why did King David break the rules by eating the consecrated bread? And the priests by working on the Sabbath? I'll tell you why: Rules make terrible masters."

He's not fussing.

"Someone greater than your rule book is here, and you're looking at him. If you knew what the Scripture meant, 'I desire affection and not ritual,' you wouldn't condemn my friends."

❧

The Master steps through their enclave.

They step back numbly.

We march after our friend. We're all ears.

"There will never be a rule against walking with me and eating up my truth. Pluck handfuls of grace freely, without cost, without limit. Others will criticize because they don't understand the true nature of what pleases me. But don't be distracted. Keep eating. Keep enjoying."

I notice the sunshine again.

The grain blows gently.

The birds sing out.

Our pace picks up. Someone tests the waters by cracking a joke. Two or three chuckle, and before long we're all half giddy again.

And I suddenly realize how hungry I am.

Matthew 12:1–8

FOR REFLECTION: Do I allow the critics, who don't yet understand, to steal my freedom and joy?

SOLIDLY ON ALL FOURS

Bartholomew, to my fellow brother in the faith. Greetings in the name of the Lord Jesus to you and your whole household.

I hope this brief epistle is carried to you hastily and reliably, for I have a real story to tell you. I have walked up the familiar steps to the temple hundreds of times in my life, sometimes with you on your visits and over a dozen times with the master himself. Being in the temple with Christ is always an adventure, but what happened today has to surpass them all!

Ever since Jesus rode the donkey into the city yesterday, he has been agitated somehow. Not in the way you or I become frustrated with an ox that won't cooperate or a bad catch of fish; things bother the Master that don't annoy anyone else.

Such was our experience in the temple today. We walked through the Court of the Gentiles as usual. Jesus moved slowly, watching all the moneychangers and merchants hocking their wares. And then it was as if the anguish of God welled up within him.

Jesus moved in among the tables and began turning them upside down one and two at a time! Those who were buying fled immediately. You can imagine the scene: sheep scampering about, doves flapping and squawking, coins spilling and rolling underfoot in every direction.

But the greatest sight was the merchants. You know how they pester everyone and constantly try to take advantage of the monopoly they've established. Everyone loved seeing them get what they deserved. Here they were, their money on the ground everywhere, their animals scampering, and their birds escaping from split cages! Ah, it was an unforgettable scene: greedy businessmen watching their inventory flee with the bleating joy of freedom!

The best part was that they couldn't run and catch their property! The quiet anger of Christ had them affixed to their stools. He shut down the whole industry with the power of his presence. Then with just a few words he pegged them: "Is it not written, 'My house will be called a house of prayer for all nations?' But you have made it 'a den of robbers.'" My friend, you wouldn't have believed it. The entire temple of Herod stopped in time. Like never before, the hill of Moriah was hushed. (Afterward we reflected on it; Jesus joked that from his boyhood he had been building tables, but this was his first time to throw them around!)

Anyway, I wanted write down the things I've learned today, hoping that you'll share them with your family and the other brothers there. The work of God cannot be mixed with a love for gain. Each pursuit excludes the other. Year by year, more and more merchants have joined the ranks. Some of them used to be devout men, but they've changed. As I reported to you in earlier correspondence, we cannot serve both God and material possessions.

Let me put it this way: The currency for transacting the Lord's business is holiness and a heart devotion to God. If that's not what we're spending, then we're not really buying anything of eternal value.

As I've thought about today's lesson, I've been struck with how easily a commercial attitude invades the ministry. I even surprise myself on this point. Until Jesus got angry at it, I had come to accept profit making in the temple as unfortunate but a reality of life. I hardly noticed it anymore. Isn't that frightening? We become blind to wrongdoing that happens right under our noses!

It seems to me now that when doing God's work, one has to be overly cautious not to get drawn away from the true focus. In fact, we must examine *every day* the purpose of our "table" of service. If we find our work polluted, even a little, it *must* be overturned.

Jesus has said that if my eye offends me I should pluck it out. I've learned another lesson today: If my ministry table offends God, I should kick the legs off!

Finally, I've been struck with the sheer force of Christ's anger. Over these months I've seen him tolerate so much personal abuse and false accusation. But tampering with the worship of his Father is obviously something he will not stand for. After seeing what I saw today, I pray we never provoke the anger of Jesus!

Enough of my preaching. Greet all the brethren.

Mark 11:15–18

FOR REFLECTION: Do my ministry efforts include any hidden profit-making motives?

CHAPTER EIGHT

IMAGINE HIM CRYING FOR YOU

"Jesus wept." Short and to the point. (It's John 11:35.)

Why? Was the fact that Jesus cried so natural and uneventful that it didn't merit anything more than a simple statement of having occurred? Or was it something John the Apostle felt inappropriate to dwell on, something he felt duty bound to mention but (as a rough and rugged "Son of Thunder") preferred to leave without elaboration?

I don't know.

"Jesus wept." How do you suppose he wept? Did he bawl like a baby, the way other big men do, with deep sobs and a lot of vocal wailing? Was he a borrow-a-handkerchief-from-your-neighbor kind of weeper? Or did he cry more discreetly? Did he shed more dignified tears? More urbane? Is it somehow more Godlike not to get carried away in emotional crying?

I'm not sure. A lot about Jesus I do not understand, including his crying. But I have some suspicions.

I suspect it was not that unusual for Jesus to cry. For one thing, he was Jewish. My perception is that most Jews feel little restraint when it comes to crying. (Their emotional abandon is one of their strengths.) For another thing, he was human. Normal humans cry. I like to think he cried somewhat regularly, because it gives me courage to cry more and not feel foolish when I do.

Another suspicion I have is that when Jesus cried, he really cried. I don't think his crying amounted to merely dabbing a tear out of the corner of his eye. ("Oh my, how foolish of me. So sorry.") No, I think he was more the nose-getting-red, tears-down-the-beard, wipe-off-the-face-with-the-back-of-the-hand, no-apologies-needed-or-offered type of crier.

I actually have some biblical evidence for this latter hypothesis. Some onlookers saw Jesus cry after Lazarus died, and their comment was, "See how he loved him!" (John 11:36) They concluded from the way Jesus cried that he loved Lazarus a great deal.

So you tell me. Did Jesus dab at a single tear, or was he messy? I vote for messy.

And because of that I like him all the more.

CLOSER THAN BROTHERS

I'm not as cynical as some people think. Just analytical.

Even about death. I find myself wondering at times what it will be like. What will I experience right after I die? What will others say about me when I'm gone? How will my family get along without me? Questions like that.

I've pondered the subject more than usual these days because of the experience with Lazarus a few days ago. Jesus received word from Mary and Martha that Lazarus was sick. The Lord wanted to go to Judea and help them. When I heard about it, I wondered why Jesus would want to return to the place he was nearly stoned to death. I hid my anxiety about the whole thing under a bad joke, something to the effect of, "Sure, let's go to Jerusalem and die right along with Lazarus." (Maybe I *am* cynical.)

But in retrospect, I'm glad for the ordeal. Mostly because it helped me see Jesus in a new light. Many who can woo a crowd with a fiery speech are ill at ease when put in an emotional situation with one or two people. Not so with Christ. You would have thought he was Lazarus's closest brother. It was as if he forgot who he was. And so did everyone else.

As I've thought about it, I find it interesting that Jesus wept but not for reasons that you or I would weep. For example, he didn't weep because he had lost a good friend forever. Nor did he cry because his dear friends Martha and Mary would now have to live without their brother. I know these weren't the reasons because Jesus already knew that Lazarus would come back to life.

Neither did Jesus cry tears of disappointment, grieving the fact that he had arrived too late to heal Lazarus. Fact is, he wasn't disappointed with his late arrival. No, he had *planned* to come late enough so he could perform a resurrection rather than a healing! (Come to think of it, Jesus was never late to anything.)

So why did Jesus cry that way, so unrestrained and unashamed? I'm still pondering that one. What I've come up with so far is this: Jesus knew that the miracle was not painless. He knew—and felt—that just because the Father is glorified does not mean that we escape sadness, grief, and even agony.

And so, I think Jesus wept out of empathy.

He felt sad that Lazarus had to endure the pain of a prolonged illness. Sad that his friend had to experience the release of his health and even his life. Lazarus had to let go of memories that would never be. The master seemed to understand the loss, though he had never endured it himself.

And I think Jesus hurt with Mary and Martha because they both agonized as to why he hadn't come sooner. *(What's taking him so long? It's never taken him this much time before. And this is an emergency!)* Each of them greeted Jesus with the same sense of crushed hope: "Lord, if you had been here, my brother would not have died!" Jesus saw that he had disappointed them. And perhaps he was humbled by their total faith in his ability to turn any hopeless situation into something good. And it moved him to tears.

If I were Lazarus, I would be proud that it happened to me. Proud that the Lord empathized that way with my family.

I hope Jesus isn't too far away when I die.

John 11:1–44

FOR REFLECTION: Do I accept the comfort of knowing that Jesus empathizes deeply with the pain I feel, even (and especially) when that pain results from the work he's doing in my life?

I HAVE NOT FORGOTTEN MY PLANS

He saw her and wept over her:

"O my beloved, how often I wanted to gather your children together, as a hen gathers her brood under her wings. When you began, you held such potential for beauty and faithfulness. I dreamed of how righteous you might be.

"But you lusted after foreigners. You let them come to your perfumed bed, letting yourself be defiled by them, ending up despising them.

"You have become desecrated by the idols you have made. You flaunt your objects of false worship for all to see.

"Your rulers have treated the fatherless and widows with contempt. You give ear to slanderous tongues. You are bloody, and you take bribes to shed blood.

"You have allowed your aliens to be oppressed; neighbors injure neighbors for profit. You have passively watched lewd acts; the nakedness of fathers you have tolerated. A man uncovers his neighbor's wife, or even his sister, and you have not abhorred it.

"My holy days are profaned. You have forgotten me.

"If you could only see yourself the way I see you. You lie naked, bruised and helpless, used up by everyone who wanted any sensual or monetary pleasure. Your sons and daughters are taken away. Your past lovers have left you in shame, your ears and nose removed, without a trace of beauty. You have paid the price of your lewdness.

"I have smitten my hand at your dishonesty. Your heart cannot endure; your hands cannot hold on in the days of my dealing with you. The nations mock your fall.

"Your eyes are shut; your head is covered. Yes, your prophets and seers are in a spirit of deep sleep.

"But hear, when all your lovers are gone, and they have finished with you, I will take you back, for I remember my plans for you. I know the beauty you possess.

"It will be that when no stone is left on another, then you will turn back to me. When you have been humbled, then you can begin to rebuild.

"I will be your Cornerstone. I am costly, but I will be freely and wholly yours, firmly placed. Believe in me, and you will not be disturbed. Build on me, and your foundation will not falter. Justice will be your measuring line and righteousness your level.

"In that day I will not cry. I will come to you, and truly you will say, 'Hosanna to the Son of David. My Prince has come.'"

Luke 19:41–44; Ezekiel 22:1–16; 23:11–28

FOR REFLECTION: How does Christ weep for my city? How do I weep?

CHAPTER NINE

IMAGINE HIM TRAINING YOU

The tutelage of Jesus Christ is transformational. It requires learning to think differently than we naturally think and learning to feel as we do not naturally feel.

Christ's training runs counter to the principles of our traditions and commonly accepted standards. It takes reasonably competent people and exposes raw inability and weakness.

In short, the training of Jesus Christ leaves nothing unchanged. It's revolutionary.

And therefore, by nature, it is humbling. When we truly submit to Christ's regimen, our bastions of pride eventually come down. Capabilities formerly clung to for security surrender to an admission of total need.

So completely must the trainee let go of himself that in the end he will know that he is fully trained when he looks into the mirror of his life and sees Jesus.

HIGH-STAKES DISCIPLESHIP

If one word could have described my life, it would have been "busy." I had been buried to the gills in activities. I was a factory of one, churning out results and tired to the core because of it.

But something was missing: I longed to be part of a miracle. I wanted my work and my life to have God's signature on it. His distinctive mark. I wanted people to observe my life and react, "My, your God is really something!"

Apparently Jesus wanted the same thing for me because he called me away from my routine to a different place. He called me to an isolated area so that he and I might rest together.

During one of our conversations, I told the Lord that I desired to impact a large number of people for him, even though I was just one rather insignificant person. Again, his thinking and mine seemed to follow the same lines. In fact, even while we were talking, people began to gather around us. They came and kept coming, and before long I was literally amazed at the size of the curious crowd that had appeared out of nowhere.

We ministered together, the Lord and I. It was a fruitful time. People enjoyed it. Time wore on, and the people stayed, wanting more.

In fact, the longer they stayed, the greater their needs seemed to be. "Lord, have you noticed that these people have needs we have not met? And frankly, there's no way we can. There are too many of them, and they have too many needs."

I thought my observation would really strike a chord of agreement with Jesus, but he acted as if I had not told him anything he didn't already know. I may be wrong, but it actually seemed as if he was simply waiting for me to mention it so he could reply, "*You* meet their need." Which is exactly what he said.

"What?" *He must not have understood me.* "I can't possibly satisfy them. Like I said, their need is simply too great."

I sent my mind in search of other reasonable reasons: "Plus we have no resources. We have nothing to work with. We're helpless, and the situation is hopeless."

He quibbled with my definition of "nothing."

"Well, all right then, we aren't down to *absolutely* nothing. Just *practically* nothing."

He seemed to be steering me like a ship when he said, "And it seems impossible, does it?"

"Yes, Lord. The impossibility of the situation is confirmed by the history of previous, similar circumstances, by the immensity of the need that looms before us, and by the depleted condition of any resources we can muster. Success is clinically impossible."

"Good! We're ready then. Bring what little you have, and let's pray."

Pray? Wouldn't it be wiser to pray if there were half a chance of an answer? Why pray if I have no faith?

"If you must pray, Lord, at least do it privately. That way we protect our reputation if nothing happens. If we let others know we're praying, then we'll build up their expectations."

"Yes, that's the idea."

"But if we fail, we'll be completely embarrassed."

"Right."

I felt the whole situation was getting out of hand. I was getting increasingly uncomfortable and told him so.

"I thought you wanted your life to be a miracle," was his comeback. "Wasn't it you who wanted people to remark at the greatness of your God?"

I affirmed my identity and claimed ownership of the words. But I argued that he hadn't given me time to prepare, that this miracle-in-the-making was catching me off guard.

"That's when miracles happen," he explained. He told me to get accustomed to being inadequate if I wanted to experience more of his power.

"You mean this is a normal way to feel in the miracle life? That if I want to go further with you, I need to get used to this?"

Is it possible for excitement to mix with fear? If so, his reply accomplished it: "Your impact is greatest when your resources are fewest. Let's pray."

He prayed. Publicly, for all to hear.

And the provision began. Slowly at first. (I wondered if he had expected a better response, but he didn't seem anxious.) Once it started, the supply multiplied into superabundance. It was nothing short of amazing.

Some in the crowd struck me as "chronic needers" (you know the kind). Even *they* were completely satisfied. Some of them came to me and said, "My, your God is really something."

I watched Jesus move among the people as they left.

That's his way, isn't it? He's at his best when we've completely depleted our resources. His specialty is bringing a disproportionately large impact out of a ridiculously paltry supply.

I grinned within. I too had been completely satisfied.

My Lord really is *something.*

Luke 9:10–17

FOR REFLECTION: Do I believe in a Jesus who has all the resources I need just for the asking?

HAM OR BEEF?

I close the door of the house with my mind once again puzzled over Jesus' words. My assumptions have been jostled. My categories badly battered.

No one ever said it in so many words, but while I was growing up, our religious traditions were top priority. We took it for granted that our practices agreed with God's commands. But the Lord has me wondering...seriously wondering.

Life according to code has always been quite comfortable. Answers were pat and predictable. Surprises were few. No wrestling with difficult choices. Just follow the tradition. Take the word of your predecessors as gospel.

There's very little wind swirling in a good, tight box.

So why is Jesus disturbing mine? "The traditions of men must surrender to the commands of God." Could I be the only disciple still struggling with this issue?

I find my place at the table along with Jesus and the others.

I've been blind to a lot of things, I guess. Like what he said about food. I've always been taught that sin launches its assault against me from the outside. Eat the right foods, drink the right drinks (avoid the wrong ones, of course), and you stay on God's good side. What could make more sense than that?

But now he says I've had it all wrong. That sin doesn't result from what I put in my stomach but from what I produce from my heart! This is beyond me.

I wait for an opening in the discussion:

"So, Lord, are you saying that *all* food is clean?"

"That's right, Simon."

"You mean to say that we can eat or drink anything we want and not commit a sin?"

"Yes. That's what I mean."

"How could you have a kingdom that doesn't restrict us from eating certain foods? Every religion prescribes those things. People will expect the same from you."

"My kingdom will break a lot of expectations. It isn't focused on eating and drinking. What matters to me is righteousness, peace, and joy in the Holy Spirit."

I look around the table at the faces of my fellows. Their interest in my line of questioning spurs me on: "So, Lord, let me see if I'm getting this right. We can eat anything we want."

"Right."

"And it doesn't matter where we eat it or who sees us?"

"I didn't say that. Ha! 'The Zealot' fits you perfectly, dear friend."

Good. Now he'll backtrack and bring some sense to this discussion. He just has *to keep some discipline in the ranks. I know people. They can't handle life without a code of conduct.*

The teacher recognizes an opportunity. "There's nothing about food or drink that's inherently sinful. Enjoy them in the true spirit of my kingdom. But as you do, remember that you're not alone in this world. Others have different opinions about food and drink. You need to be aware of that."

"But how do we know when and where to partake or refrain?"

"In everything, be guided by love."

Wait a minute. He isn't retreating. This still sounds wishy-washy. Give us some rules, Lord. What days of the week are forbidden? What kinds of food shouldn't we eat? What kinds of drinks must we avoid? Love is good for forgiving and reconciling and such. But it doesn't speak the language of decision-making.

"Let me give you three principles to show you how love should guide you. The first is the principle of freedom. You are free in your relationship with me to enjoy whatever food or drink you want to. There is no sin in the thing itself. Don't criticize a brother who makes a decision different than yours, and no one should criticize you for your choices either."

Sounds like love of self to me....

"What's wrong with loving yourself, Simon?"

(No answer.) *Did I say something?*

"The second principle is that of responsibility. If a brother sees you doing something which your freedom has permitted you to do, and he's genuinely offended by it, then you're responsible for loving him by curbing your own freedom. Either stop partaking, or find times and ways of enjoying your freedom that do not violate the love of the brethren."

"Lord, these are difficult principles to apply. There are so many different viewpoints on hundreds of issues. And every community has its own issues and viewpoints."

"Yes, Simon, but I will help you. And there's a third guideline I want you to use in dealing with the difficulty of these decisions. It's the principle of personal faith. At times you will not be completely sure of what to do. You'll wonder what others would think or say if they knew how you felt. In those situations you can only hold up your decision before the Father. Ask him honestly to show you the way to go. If your conscience is clear before him, then seize by faith your freedom in the context of your personal relationship with him, not forgetting the principle of responsibility, of course."

"Lord, pardon me for belaboring the point. You've given us principles instead of prescriptions. Some of us do better with legislation. We're used to it. For those of us who aren't too good at applying principles, do you have a backup program we could use?"

"A child needs to be told every little thing to do or avoid, Simon. But there comes a time when a child grows to the age where he shouldn't be given rules anymore. To do so would hinder his progress toward maturity.

By giving you principles, I'm treating you not as children but as brothers and friends. I'm giving you the freedom and responsibility to decide for yourselves."

"It's just that the rules, though confining, were somehow easier than what you're suggesting."

"I know, my zealous friend. Living by principles forces you to think. It forces you to depend on me. And that's the whole point, isn't it?"

Mark 7:1–23; Romans 14:1–23

FOR REFLECTION: Do I allow the principles of freedom, responsibility, and personal faith to guide my decision-making process? Or do I still tie myself to rules and regulations because it seems an easier, more comfortable way of relating to God?

TRANSFIGURATION

"That was glorious! I've never seen anything like that in all my life!" Peter blinked his eyes deliberately as if to check that they were still in working order.

"Incredible!" James concurred. "This is historic: Jesus, Moses, and Elijah all appearing together in such brilliance. I just regret that only three of us saw it."

Peter's ingenuity was already in full stride: "There may be something we can do about that. We should build three tents to preserve what has happened here. That way the blessing will continue."

"And others could come and see it," agreed James. "They could take a bit of the glory home with them. Those who heard about it would get so excited they would come here to the mountain to see it for themselves."

John had listened to all this and was not so enthusiastic. "What if the glory doesn't stay in the tents? What if it fades?"

James quickly responded, "The people would benefit from even a small portion of what we've seen. They wouldn't have to experience the full glory to be blessed. And how would they know it was fading anyway?"

"Besides," added Peter, "we would have the original tents still here. The people could come and see where it all happened. It would be a kind of shrine."

"Or here's another idea," suggested James. "Perhaps we could reproduce in other places the kind of wonder that happened here. If we can remember exactly what we did to make the glory appear here on the mountain, we could produce it again elsewhere."

Peter was intrigued and pursued the suggestion. "We know it was just the three of us. We know we were praying—"

"Be honest," John interrupted. "We were sleeping when it happened. Fact is, we had nothing to do with the appearance of the glory."

"Yes, I suppose you're right."

"What we might do, however," countered John, being pulled into the spirit of the discussion, "is analyze what happened in hopes that we might predict when and where Jesus will do it again."

"Then we could have more people in place to enjoy the experience," agreed his brother.

"All right," said Peter, the leader, "I think we have a plan then. We want to capitalize on every advantage for the cause of Christ, not overlooking any available resource."

Just then a cloud moved swiftly over them and engrossed them. So rapidly did it come that it acted like a giant cloth, wiping away the plans they had been sketching.

Then a booming voice said, as if to etch permanently in their minds a better plan: "This is my beloved Son in whom I am well pleased. Hear him."

A picture of God's desire now appeared before them. Moses had gone. Elijah had returned to his place. Only Jesus remained. Not the dazzling Jesus but the same friend who had walked and talked with Peter and the others. Not the attraction in light, but the same one who shared with them daily truths to live by.

And it suddenly became clear to them. Peter was the first to make the admission. "I can't believe it. We have the very Son of God with us, yet we had begun to revere something that had happened in the past."

"Not only revere," agreed James, "but we were planning ways to preserve or reproduce the glory ourselves. We were letting our eyes be drawn away from Christ and what he might want to do next."

"Deadly," agreed John. "Dim reflections of past glory are a poor substitute for experiencing God's surprises."

Peter went on, "It's as if we thought this was the pinnacle of God's creativity, when in fact he may have even greater things in store for us."

"When you think of it," pondered James, loosening his legs for the descent, "we need to remember the lesson from the manna in the ancient wilderness: If you try to hoard God's blessings, they spoil."

"Mmm, good analogy. How about this: The Bread of life is best when it's fresh."

Matthew 17:1–8

FOR REFLECTION: What "shrines" have I built that hinder my ability to expect something new and different that Jesus may want to do today?

CHAPTER TEN

IMAGINE HIM REBUKING YOU

Would Jesus feel comfortable in your church?

Not if he came in the robes and sandals of first-century Middle East, but if he put on the average clothing of a middle-aged man in your church, groomed himself in the typical way, and just slipped in unobtrusively and anonymously as a visitor? Would he feel comfortable among you? Would a few people shake his hand with a smile?

What do you suppose he would think during the singing? Or the announcements? Would the preaching please him? What would he think as he heard about your ministries? Your missionaries? Still more important, what would he sense in the "heart" of the congregation? What attitudes would he detect?

Or consider this: Would Jesus feel comfortable in your home? Same situation, as an unidentified and average guest. What "vibes" would he pick up, what words would he hear? What would he think as he listened to you interact with other family members and friends? As he shared in your entertainment?

Interesting food for thought, isn't it?

WHEN PRIDE SPEAKS

"The euphoria of a great moment can bring on the embarrassment of a great mistake."

Peter had done it again—dropped a verbal stone that virtually begged us to ask for more. It was after our Love Feast at Nathan and Rachel's house in the old quarter. As had become our custom as a church, the men were in the kitchen washing the dishes and listening to the women make jokes about us from the sitting room. *They may tease us, but they love the effort we make.*

Peter's "baited hook" arose as we discussed the issue of rebuke and correction. (We had in our house fellowship one husband who had an ongoing problem with anger toward his wife and kids. We were wondering how to approach such a delicate subject.)

I considered myself doubly fortunate: to have one of the great apostles as my pastor and also to be in the same home fellowship with him. Needless to say, I never missed.

"Have I ever told you fellows about one of the worst days of my life?" Peter continued.

I was sure he had. (Forgetfulness was increasing with his years.) It was either the denial or the "Satan episode." But he always told his stories with a new slant, and hearing his accounts made me feel closer to my master, whom I had never met in the flesh. In fact, we all felt the same way, so we customarily left a silence that indicated we had not heard the story before or at least not recently enough.

It worked.

"We were near Caesarea Philippi. I remember walking along the river when the Lord threw out one of those questions that had an innocent surface covering a potentially mysterious interior."

So that's where he learned the skill.

Shem nudged me as a reminder to keep working on the dishes.

"Anyway, Jesus asked us what people were saying about him—who they thought the Son of Man was. I thought it over silently while John and Thomas gave him an update on what they had heard.... Can somebody take this towel for me; I'm afraid I'm going to drop something, and then Mama won't let me hang out with the boys anymore!"

Pastor, now released from cleanup, found a nearby stool.

"Well, then the Lord put the question to *us*. Who did *we* think he was? You fellows know me; you only need to call me to feeding time once, and even then a whisper will do. I seized the opening: I said he was the Christ, the Son of the living God!"

The rest of us could not restrain our laughter of amusement (at the way he said it) and admiration (for his being the one there at the right time with the right words).

"Then I received the compliment of a lifetime. He blessed me for my insight. Of course, it was not *my* thought. We all understood that. He went on to say that the truth of my confession about his character would be the foundation of his church."

The apostle stood and walked to the other side of the room, a painful memory invading his expression.

"Brothers, do you remember last month when I preached about spiritual gifts? I made the point that every gift has its potential hazard. I learned that truth the hard way. I have the gift of leadership. Someone like me, enabled by God to lead, has the confidence to know what should be done and how best to do it. The problem is that someone like me also can easily step over the line, pridefully thinking that I know better than anyone else how to lead. Does that make any sense?"

Group affirmation. No one wanted to sidetrack him with a question.

"I learned this lesson the hard way, which takes me back to my story. I still had my head in the clouds of euphoria when Jesus began telling us again that we should not tell others his identity. I was bounding with confidence and began to wonder if Jesus planned to go into hiding for a while. Naturally the thought crossed my mind that he might call upon my leadership abilities to represent his interests with certain local officials, as well as to head up the growing band of disciples for him. So you can imagine how upset I was whenever he would bring up the subject of his death...which he did that very day. And something snapped inside of me.

"Jesus seemed to be giving up. He could be so bold when it was *our* dilemma, *our* empty nets, or *our* desire to heal someone. But when it came to *himself,* he seemed so often like a seed waiting to wither up and die, to fall safely to the ground and hide. I couldn't stand it. I would see to it myself that he succeeded. I would have no part in such pessimistic talk.

"And I told him so."

Uncomfortable silence.

"You guys think *I* can give a firm rebuke; I don't get anywhere *near* the righteous indignation of Christ! 'Out of your sight, Lord? No problem. Give me something, *anything* to hide behind!'"

Thank goodness for Peter's sense of humor. We needed an excuse to relieve some of our tension, and we took it.

"I felt about every emotion you can feel: anger, shock, embarrassment. The worst thing was that I knew instantly he was right. I hadn't been thinking about what the Father's plan might be. I was only concerned about how the Lord's future impacted my security and status."

He perused our faces and apparently sensed trustworthiness. "Let me share something very personal with you men. It took me quite a while to recover from his calling me Satan. That hit me very hard. But in time I began to see that he wasn't calling me, Peter, a name. He was trying to show me that my selfish thinking and my prideful words were from the pit where Satan dwells. If it's not holy, it's hellish.

"Last year I wrote a circular letter to the brethren scattered abroad. One of the ways I counseled them was to be humble before God so that he can lift them up at the proper time.

"Well, I've got a 'kitchen-crew version' for you: If you *exalt* yourself under the mighty hand of God, he will *humble* you in due time!"

Said as only Peter can.

"And take my word for it, guys. Both versions are true, but the kitchen edition hurts a lot more. So hand me one of those towels, will you? I need to polish up on my servanthood!"

Matthew 16:13–23; 1 Peter 5:6

FOR REFLECTION: Do I work harder at humbling myself or exalting myself? (Would Jesus be convinced by my proof?)

A DIFFERENT BREED

Eight men sit around a small fire in a leper colony, warming themselves and talking:

"I agree with you completely, Stephen. The living conditions in this hole are deplorable. When in the world will we get some attention to this situation?"

"Maybe we ought to lodge a formal complaint that the colony elders aren't doing their jobs. Those guys are too old; they've completely lost touch with the people's needs. All they care about is that they've locked up their positions for the foreseeable future."

"Speaking of out of touch, do you guys know that I haven't had a visit from any of my relatives in over two weeks! When I first came here, someone came by every day to bring me something. Now I'm just begging like the rest of you scroungers."

"Yeah, I'm equally important to my relatives, it seems. I heard through Gehazi that my brothers are pestering my wife for their portion of my inheritance. What am I, dead already? Considerate imbeciles, aren't they!"

"You're getting the kind of treatment you deserve, Benjamin. How many times have we tolerated your nonstop boasting about how you cheated them out of the family cows? 'More power to them' I say, and when you finally die, one of your filthy brothers will get the privileges of your wife's bedroom as well. How do you feel about that, you good for nothing—"

"Curse you, Ethan. My business is my—"

"All right, you two. Leave it alone. Anyway, here comes Assir. We haven't seen him in a while. Probably owes me some money."

"Greetings, Assir! Where have you been? We thought maybe you wouldn't be coming back to join us anymore."

"No, I'm back."

"Where have you been?"

"Here and there, that's all."

"You don't look so well, Assir."

"No worse than the rest of you I'd say. None of you should talk."

"No offense intended, my friend. Just an observation, that's all. Say, how long has it been since we were all together anyway?"

"Not long enough..."

"Feeling's mutual, Stephen."

"Well, let's see, I think it has been about three months."

"Yes, of course. The last time we were all together was the day that healer came through. Remember that?"

"That's right. We sure fell for that guy, didn't we? Thought things were really going to change."

"I saw through him from the beginning. I just went along with the rest of you out of boredom."

"Yeah, right, Ethan. You're never wrong are you, you—"

"Hey, wait a minute! Do you guys remember that half-breed that tagged along with us then? Wasn't he there that day?"

"I remember him, but I sure don't miss him."

"Anybody seen the guy?"

"Nope, haven't seen him."

"Me neither."

"Strange. Just disappeared."

"Ah, who cares. He was always different from us anyway."

Luke 17:11–19

FOR REFLECTION: Have I become "infected" with ingratitude? And if so, am I getting any therapy for this malady?

MARTHA'S SONG

Martha intended the day to be a lip-smacking concoction, one that she could savor for years to come. All the ingredients were on hand: rare opportunity, wide impact, great challenge, special guest.

But the recipe had flopped. How could it have gone so wrong?

She lay awake in her bed. Her sister seemed to be up, moving about in another part of the house. *I find it hard to care about her just now.* But Martha lay still, tears soaking her pillow.

O Lord, why are you so far from saving me?
As hard as I try, I seem the least of your favorites.
I cry out to you by day, but you seem not to hear;
I cry out at night, and it's as if you don't understand.

I'm so sorry I got carried away;
I lost perspective yet again.
You were right to rebuke my agitation;
how do I end up ignoring the very One I want to please?

I guess I wonder why you gave me so much energy
if I can't use it to bring a smile to your face?
And why did you create me to love a job well done,
if it doesn't bring some pleasure to your day?

And then the Spirit of the Lord reached out to minister to her.

My dear, dear Martha, I couldn't love you more;
I'd give my very life to save your soul.

Please don't misunderstand the words I said to you today;
I can't tell you what it meant to be invited to your home.

The meal you set before me was exquisitely prepared;
I enjoyed the way you brought it all together nice and hot.
You really have a gift for making people feel at ease,
so I bless you for your ministry today.

The only plea I offer is that you give me something more;
I appreciate your talents, but I love who you are.
In your whirlwind of activity, don't withhold the better gift.
It's the sweet and precious person behind the things you do.

Then Martha fell asleep. She dreamed, and in her dream…
There was a flock of sheep;
    they had roamed all day over rocky terrain.
During the night there was a terrible storm;
    it brought strong rain and blowing wind.
The shepherd brought the sheep against
    a wall of rock for protection,
    but still the sheep had to work hard
        to keep from being blown over.
By morning, the storm had passed.
The shepherd led the flock to green pastures
    of lush grass.
    The sun was out.
There was a slow-moving stream,
    with refreshing water to drink.

By and by, the shepherd himself sat down nearby,
    not in any hurry.
After the sheep had had their fill of nourishment and drink,
    they lay down in the warm grass.
        They slept,
            peacefully.
The shepherd played soothing melodies
    on his stringed instrument,
    and sang familiar words
        which they had all heard before.
The sun shone down on them,
    and they were warm and safe.

Martha slept peacefully, a slight smile curving the corner of her mouth. Her pillow was dry. Tomorrow would not be as busy as she had planned.

Luke 10:38–42

FOR REFLECTION: Am I letting myself get hurried out of Jesus' presence these days?

WATCH AND PRAY

Several of us had been discussing prayer, wanting to understand better how to draw on its power, wanting to be more skillful at it. In fact, so united were we in this desire that we wondered if the Lord wasn't somehow calling us to a higher level of prayerfulness.

So we decided to meet regularly to study aspects of prayer. We planned to hold discussions on it, and we sincerely asked the Lord to reveal to us new insights on how to pray.

But as we began meeting, we had trouble overcoming a certain heaviness in our group. We prayed for joy, but our thoughts seemed stuck in the quagmire of pessimism. We began, for example, to dwell on the rebelliousness of some young people we knew. We brought up the number of families that were being severed by parents who paid more attention to their careers than to their spouses and children. We lamented the condition of the church, how apathy and tolerance of falsehood ran rampant.

(Why doesn't the Lord come and deliver us from this negativism? This group needs some grief counseling! Isn't prayer supposed to bring us the victory?)

Rather than spend much time on these depressing issues, we tended to pray about lighter matters, thinking that a few answered prayers would buoy our group. But the heaviness lingered.

After a few weeks we discussed our frustrations with the whole experience, wondering if the Lord had really led us to pursue prayer after all. We considered disbanding but felt we should try to end on a high note rather than during a time of discouragement. So we recommitted to another period of discussions.

This proved a mistake. All sorts of problems cropped up, this time within our little group. Feelings were hurt. Some became critical of others, questioning motives and such. At times one or another would dominate the group or alternatively would withdraw into silence for no apparent reason. Occasionally we would compare our group with others, sometimes bragging about our strengths, at other times feeling discouraged about our weaknesses.

It seemed as if prayer had become a fertile ground planted liberally with the seeds of temptation. Our hearts had been in the right place, but our propensity to sin was stronger.

We were at another crisis point. Had this been a bad idea from the beginning? The prayer insights we had hoped for had eluded us. ("Maybe we need some guest speakers.") Turmoil in the group, compounded by personal struggles within the members themselves, proved to be high hurdles to our progress.

(Why does the Lord allow so many problems to plague us this way? Doesn't he know that we could proceed with our learning if we could focus on prayer instead of struggling so much?)

A turnaround never seemed to come for our group. We were unable to climb out of the valley.

Finally it was as if everyone simultaneously sensed that we needed to quit meeting. The time just seemed right.

Someone joked that it was a good thing Jesus still prays, because if it were all up to us, there would be a serious prayer deficit!

That got me wondering if our prayer group had missed something. We had wanted to learn how to pray, but would we have been better off simply joining in with the praying that Jesus wanted to do through us? Were the burdensome problems that depressed us actually his burdens? Did he want us to feel what he was feeling about sin?

And the temptations we struggled against—could they have been part of what he wanted us to learn about prayer? Maybe those were wake-up calls to help us see that Satan knows how powerful prayer can be, reminders that our sinful nature is never so active as when we try to pray.

But why did our call to prayer end as clearly as it had begun? (The Lord didn't seem to be angry with us.) Had the issue somehow been resolved? Had Jesus gotten his result? Had the solution been set in motion?

My reflections led me to believe that maybe Jesus had been trying to teach us to pray after all. In fact, it seems he was working harder at teaching than we were at learning.

Lectures on prayer would perhaps have made things clearer, but what he gave us was much more intriguing. His kind of prayer demanded listening to him. Sensing his burdens. Seeing that our flesh always rises up to thwart prayerfulness. Knowing the times. It meant praying when the battle rages, praising when the struggle is won, moving into action when he gives the signal.

I guess what we had wanted was prayer principles.

What he wanted was prayer partners.

Matthew 26:36–46

FOR REFLECTION: Am I paying attention to the ways Jesus wants to involve me in his prayer life?

CHAPTER ELEVEN

IMAGINE HIM CALLING YOU

The problem with the New Testament is that its writings fail to recognize the optional nature of Christ's lordship. This can be traced back to the fact that Jesus was similarly misinformed.

Would that the New Testament writers could have understood what many generations of believers have since discovered: that it is quite possible, even popular, to receive the comfort of having a Savior without going through the cumbersome process of living according to his commands. Many of us have become quite proficient at living this way. We debate the issue, wondering why the New Testament doesn't seem to agree with itself, wishing its writers had cleared up this dilemma.

Why the oversight of biblical inspiration?

The reason is (and here I remove my tongue from my cheek) that generations of anemic commitment to Christ have created a brand of Christianity that shouldn't exist. It's abnormal. From Jesus' perspective, trusting him as Savior automatically demands a commitment to him as Lord.

New Testament believers knew this instinctively. Society in New Testament times was not friendly to the Christian faith. Jerusalem, Ephesus, Athens—they and many others rose up to snarl at members of The Way.

Some believers in subsequent centuries couldn't afford to consider

Christ as anything but Lord. The cities that sought to snuff them out had names like Moscow and Beijing. Those brothers and sisters in Christ clearly understood the meaning of the gospel the way the New Testament saints did, because to align themselves with Christ exacted a toll. To willingly endure such persecution, they had to *know* Jesus is Lord over all.

Is lordship optional for a Christian? The question only arises for those who live in a time and place where Christianity is culturally acceptable, where they have enough resources and support to simulate true Christianity without having to cling every day to Jesus for emotional, spiritual, and even physical survival.

So what do we do, those of us who have the option of choosing "armchair Christianity," if we are to live the way Jesus intended us to live?

We could all move to places where Christians experience persecution for their faith. Or we could pray for anti-Christian sentiment to increase where we presently live.

But these are not likely solutions for too many. For most of us there is another, much tougher solution. We can answer his call to surrender to his lordship even though few around us do so, even though we do not have outward persecution to teach us how to be more committed. We can draw so close to Jesus that we see the same sin and spiritual resistance that he sees in us and in our surroundings.

In short, we can live more like Jesus. (Remember, his lordship became an issue no matter where he went, even in the sleepiest village.) If we live more like him, we might find that we don't have time to discuss whether or not he's Lord as well as Savior.

We'll be living proof.

A FORK IN THE ROAD

Envision yourself at a fork in the road.

You first look at the path on the left. Due to the multitude that have traveled it, it's quite wide. The sheer number of people who have chosen it causes you to assume outright that the leftward way is the correct way. *Isn't it usually the case that the majority know the best route most of the time?*

For little other reason than curiosity you glance at the other path, the one to the right. Of necessity, it is narrow. The very scarcity of those traveling it reinforces your earlier conviction that it's the wrong way to go. *Is it not true that in only a few instances a few people take a little-used route and end up where they want to go?*

So narrow is this second path that only one person can travel it at a time. And from where you stand, you can see that the path is already occupied. Jesus Christ stands on the path, just a short distance from the fork. There's a cross at his feet. His message is clear: "Come this way."

Of course you begin to consider reasons for turning to the right, reasons for taking a route that most others deliberately declined. So you look to see what the narrow path holds in store for those who choose it. (Jesus makes no attempt to hide any part of the path.) Clearly this path leads to suffering, rejection, and death.

"Lord, it looks like you have chosen the narrow path."

"Yes, I have."

"If you see as clearly as I do that this path leads to hardship and eventually death, I am wondering why you've chosen to walk it anyway."

He says to you, "Look farther ahead." (You do.) "You see, this path leads to resurrection."

Suddenly you realize that it would have been much easier if you hadn't glanced to the right at all. You'd have no decision to make; you could, without a second thought, join the others.

You look back to the wide way, wondering where it would lead. It leads to gratification, which explains why those traveling it feel they've made the right choice. It explains the width.

Train your eyes farther up the left road. Where does it lead? You strain to see that far. It seems faint and unclear. *No wonder those on the wide road don't look ahead. It's difficult to see clearly. One feels almost blindfolded.*

"It leads to destruction." You hear Jesus' voice again. A compassionate voice filled with regret. "They are gaining the world but losing their own souls."

Where's the profit in that?

"So, if I were to choose the narrow path, what would I have to do?"

His eyes move downward and take in the cross. "You would have to pick up that cross and join me in carrying it."

It looks very heavy to you, doubtless a two-handed job. "I'll do most of the lifting," Jesus says.

Still, I wouldn't be able to hold on to my possessions. I would have to let go of my house, my land, even my family. That would be tantamount to losing my life!

"And," Jesus continues, "you'd have to learn to walk single file—behind me."

So that's how the path stays so narrow.

At that moment you notice the reason the road forked in this particular place. Someone had decided to build a huge tower right over the old road. Apparently it was designed as a grand monument through which all would travel. But it now lay as a parable in stone, for the builder had not had the resources to finish what he had begun.

It gives you pause.

You find yourself wishing you had a third path to choose, one that was medium narrow, one that promised medium gain for medium sacrifice, one that might not declare you "worthy" but would at least render you "acceptable."

A different voice (whether from within you or outside it's difficult to tell) chimes in, saying that there is such a path and that it's much more comfortable.

You think about it and look up at Jesus' face. His shaking head sends the message "There is no third path."

At once the choice is painfully clear.

Can I go it alone, apart from the majority? (I can just hear their ridicule the instant I turn to the right.) And if I do, can I actually follow him? Do I have what it takes to finish? Or if I don't go to the right, am I willing to do without the words of eternal life?

"Come this way," Jesus says.

Envision yourself at that fork in the road, knowing that the path you choose will make an eternal difference.

Matthew 7:13–14; 10:34–39; Luke 9:23–26; 14:26–33; John 6:60–68
FOR REFLECTION: Do I see the two paths for what they really are?

JUST ONE OTHER THING

He was still a young man, enjoying those unforgettable years when two of life's issues seem to constantly wrestle one another: trying to make financial ends meet and facing the expanding expenses of a growing family.

Ben's ability to persevere came with the commitment to Jesus Christ which he and his wife shared. They had both come to know Christ personally and had discussed how they wanted their lives to count for the Lord's work. When the children came along, it seemed only natural to raise them according to biblical principles.

Prayer was a thread that ran through their lives. Prayer for the children as they approached school age and the accompanying challenges. Prayer for the Lord's provision for housing, first in helping them pay their rent and then in helping them buy their first small home.

Prayer that the Lord Jesus would use them in whatever way he desired:

"Lord, we're yours. Take our lives and use us in your service. We're totally available to you. Just lead us clearly. That is all we ask."

"Good, Ben, that's just the prayer I delight to hear. I can really use you as committed followers. I need to let you both know, though, that getting serious about my work isn't easy. I can't promise you the best living conditions. But I do promise that I will always meet your needs, not only for you and your wife but for your children as well."

"I appreciate your pointing out that little problem, Lord. I hadn't really thought too much about the impact on my family. In fact, as I think about it further, this may not be the best time for us to make a change, given the family needs and all. I know from your Word that if I don't provide for my family, then I'm worse than an unbeliever. I think we'd better wait until our children are out of this important age."

I'm disappointed to hear Ben say that. I have a wonderful ministry opportunity for him this year. The family would be a great asset.

"Ben, how long do you think you need to delay?"

"All I need is one year, Lord. Count on us after that."

A few years later Ben's children had grown up, left the house, and were living successfully on their own, pursuing various interests. By this time Ben had become very important in his own job, having received more and more responsibility over the years. He had also taken on a few more financial obligations and was working diligently to settle them.

The family continued to value prayer as their lifeline to God: "Lord, recently you seem to be bringing back to our minds the desire we've had over the years to serve you more fully. It appears that the timing may now be right: The family has grown up so we do not have that concern any longer. We're ready to serve you."

"That is music to my ears, Ben. There's still plenty of time for you to invest in my kingdom. Let's go."

"Great, Lord, no problem. But before we actually leave, let me wrap up just a few loose ends so that I don't leave my career obligations in a poor state of affairs. Doing so would leave a bad testimony, which I do not want to do. Plus my parents are aging, as you know. Perhaps I should wait just a bit to make sure they'll receive adequate care in their old age."

I wish Ben wouldn't make this mistake again. Especially now. The harvest is really ripe where I planned to send him. In fact, in just a month or so the spiritual climate will change, and the opportunity will be over.

"How long would it take to wrap up these responsibilities, Ben?"

"I only expect it will require a month, Lord. Then we'll be set to go."

Later on in life Ben had the satisfaction of looking back on years of good experiences. God had been faithful to him as he oversaw the days of his parents' illnesses and death. His working years had run their full course. He and his wife had many friendships which they continued to cherish.

They were thankful for how the Lord had blessed them with fine children who loved God. They often reflected on the Lord's goodness: "Jesus, we're so grateful to you for the ways you've blessed us. It might seem a bit funny to say it, but I feel we're truly free to serve you now."

"That's fine, Ben. You still have much to offer."

"Then I guess we're ready to go!"

Good! I have a job for Ben and his wife that will take only one hour. It's a short task but very important.

"Lord Jesus, we'll just say good-bye to our kids and a few friends, and then we'll be off."

"How long will the good-byes take, Ben?"

"Not more than an hour. We'll do it quickly."

"Ben, I'm afraid you don't have an hour to waste. You seem to have run out of time. It looks like you had too many reasons not to follow me."

"I'm truly sorry, Lord. I wish now that I had made some harder choices when I was younger. But you know, Lord, I have a wonderful son. I have brought him up to love you, too. Could you ask him to serve you?"

"Of course, Ben. I have been planning to do that anyway."

Ben's son was a fine Christian man, married to a lovely and godly wife. They were navigating those unforgettable years when finances were tough. Having young children stretched them, of course. But in the Lord they found strength to keep going.

One day the Lord Jesus approached Ben's son. Getting his attention, Jesus said, "Could I share with you a challenge that would be a real adventure?"

"Oh sure, Lord. I'll be right with you. Just give me a minute."

Luke 9:57–62

FOR REFLECTION: Have I established an unhealthy pattern of putting off the Lord and his work?

PART THREE

IN THE SOLITUDE OF THE NIGHT WATCHES

Eventually the story line of your relationship with Christ will enter some chapters in which you and he go through difficulties together. Tension will build and complicate matters. Hardship will push you to your limits. Or discouragement will settle in.

Such dark times offer lessons you cannot learn when the sunshine of ease beams down on your smiling face. In fact, Jesus and the life he calls us to cannot be fully understood apart from suffering. And so he bids us go deeper with him to share in his times of pain.

Some would rather avoid participation in Christ's hardships at any cost. But they pay a high price for such a choice. To shun the suffering of Christ is to lose out on an understanding of his lordship and compassion.

In some ways one can see more clearly in the dark. For during the night watches of our Savior's life, we recognize that he willingly did more for us than we ourselves would or could possibly do for anyone else. When we see him plumb the depths of humiliation, we realize the extent of his love for us.

But the night shows us even more. It shows willingness. It reveals that Jesus Christ enduring sufferings as a weakened man when he could have instantaneously escaped them as almighty God. It exposes the fact that he did not endure it all to prove to himself that he could do it. No, his motives were obedience to his Father and love for you and me.

In short, spending the lonely night watches with Christ shows us his greatness.

Do you want to feel a deeper sense of awe for your Savior? Want a chest bursting with pride for what he has done? Need a dose of true humility to counteract your own self seeking?

If so, you must be willing to meet Jesus in situations that are hard to bear. You must stick with him through times that many avoid.

To succeed in doing so, you will need a full portion of loyalty—a dogged commitment to stay by his side even when he isn't popular, even when crowds don't applaud or wave branches in celebration.

Loyalty grows when you see your Savior assaulted so viciously that you wonder if he can overcome. When your heart pounds in your chest and you wonder if you have chosen the right side. When you find your grip on Christ strained so hard that you despair of hanging on. But stay steadfast with teeth-clenching determination anyway. That's loyalty. And that's the lesson of the long night with Christ.

Especially when he proves able and faithful once again.

When dusk begins to blanket your landscape, don't lose heart. It only means that Christ is calling you to share his loneliness, his suffering. It means he's calling you to share in the very tasks his Father called him to perform: the hard tasks, the impossible and thankless tasks.

Don't despair of the darkness. To be sure, no one will congratulate you for falling into it. But the roots of your relationship with Jesus will sink even deeper as the sun sets past the horizon line. For when you obey Jesus' call to hardship, you realize you're not walking alone. You're simply walking in his footsteps.

Imitate Christ Jesus. Endure the night.

CHAPTER TWELVE

IMAGINE HIM RESISTING TEMPTATION FOR YOU

If someone challenged you to live without sin for a month but also gave you the right to define what sin is, what would you do?

If you wanted to meet the challenge, you'd probably ease up on the standard. You'd define sin in less stringent terms so you'd have half a chance of succeeding.

That's what you and I would do.

But enter Jesus. Expectations just don't work with him. He did the reverse. He made the definition tougher.

Either he had no sense, or he was a fundamentally different kind of person than you and I. Browse through the fifth chapter of Matthew's gospel and you'll see what I mean. The contemporary mores said if you hated someone so much that you murdered him, you had definitely entered sin territory (verse 21). Jesus had a good chance of steering clear of murder his whole life. If perfection was his goal, he should have left well enough alone. Instead, he made the standard tougher, asserting that common, everyday hatred pushes you over the boundary line into sin (verse 22).

Take another example. You and I would have accepted the standard "Do not commit adultery" as demanding enough (verse 27). Firm but reasonable. Jesus came along and upped the ante: "...anyone who looks at a woman lustfully has already committed adultery with her in his heart" (verse 28).

Couple this thought with a short but searching verse from the stylus of the Lord's brother: "...whoever keeps the whole law and yet stumbles at just one point is guilty of breaking all of it" (James 2:10).

Is it coming into focus? Higher demands. Margin for indiscretions, nil.

A person resisting *every* sin that tempts him is akin to someone threading a needle from forty yards away...with thirty yards of thread! Yet one man in time's chronicles managed no less: "For we do not have a high priest who is unable to sympathize with our weaknesses, but we have one who has been tempted in every way, just as we are—yet was without sin" (Hebrews 4:15).

He did it. And not just for a month. The boy stayed away from the candy. The teenager denied the lusts. The man said no to the prideful words. For a whole lifetime, Jesus resisted temptation—real, not token, temptation.

Do you know how he did it? He was motivated: He knew that every time he was tempted, your eternity hung in the balance.

ANOTHER DAY IN THE LIFE

I am a storyteller. I raise my voice to all mankind. You who are simple, gain prudence; you who are foolish, gain understanding. Listen, for I have worthy things to say; I open my lips to speak what is right. I know not if my story is true, but I know it will make your heart glad:

> At twilight, as the day was fading, as the dark of night set in, a young man walked down the street, passing by the corner where an adulteress stayed.
>
> Then out came a woman to meet him, dressed like a prostitute and with crafty intent. (Her kind is loud and raucous, or subtle and coy; she wanders about, now in the street, now in the square, lurking at every corner. Even if she returns to a husband and children, she wanders in her heart.)
>
> She took hold of the young man and kissed him, and with brazen face she said, "I have peace offerings at home; today I fulfilled my vows. So I came out to meet you. (Just you. I care for no other.)"
>
> The young man was assaulted by rationalizations. *I'm not a child anymore. This is an out-of-the-way place; no one knows me or my family here. Night is falling; I won't be seen. What could it hurt?*
>
> She pursued her prey. "I looked for you, and finally I have found you! I have covered my bed with colored linens from Egypt. I have perfumed my bed with myrrh, aloes, and cinnamon. All for you, only you."
>
> *No, not for all the pleasures of all the women in Egypt. I'll not lust after her beauty, nor let her captivate me with her eyes, for a prostitute*

reduces one to a loaf of bread, and the adulteress preys upon the very life.

Undaunted, she pulled him toward her door. "Come, let's drink deep of love till morning; let's enjoy ourselves with love!"

Can a man scoop fire into his lap without his clothes being burned? Can a man walk on hot coals without his feet being scorched? So is he who sleeps with another man's wife; no one who touches her will go unpunished.

"My husband is not at home; he has gone on a long journey. He took his purse filled with money and will not be home till full moon."

Men do not despise a thief if he steals to satisfy his hunger when he is starving. Yet if he is caught, he must pay sevenfold, though it costs him all the wealth of his house.

But a man who commits adultery lacks judgment; whoever does so destroys himself. Blows and disgrace are his lot, and his shame will never be wiped away; for jealousy arouses a husband's fury, and he will show no mercy when he takes revenge. He will not accept any compensation; he will refuse the bribe, however great it is.

She clung to her prize, almost as if she knew.

The young man turned and walked away.

Her clutch was powerless against the resolute heart. (It always is.)

The youth returned to his home in strength, carrying on his shoulders the heavy weight of the world.

O reader, rejoice! You have a great high priest who has gone through the heavens: Jesus, the Son of God. So hold firmly to the faith you possess. For you do not have a high priest who cannot sympathize with your weaknesses but one who has faced temptation in every way, just as you do. Yet he was without sin.

This has a great deal of meaning for us. But the dearest to me is this: We may approach the throne of grace with confidence so that we may receive mercy and find grace to help us in our time of need.

Thank you, young man, my God.

Proverbs 7:6–20; 6:25–35; Hebrews 4:14–16

FOR REFLECTION: How can I draw encouragement from the fact that Jesus understands the reality of the temptations I face?

THE REASON HE STOOD STRONG

Forty days and nights of fasting had accelerated Jesus' weakness to an unprecedented level of quiet need. His physical strength was wrung out of him.

Predictably, with the synchronization of a master, Satan came. The opportunity for seduction was at hand. Surely now the Son of God couldn't resist the urge to indulge in his power.

Surely he couldn't resist the temptation to turn a stone into fresh warm bread. "Go ahead, you deserve it. No one else could have lasted forty days. I won't tell anyone that it was my suggestion. It'll be our little secret. You *can* do it, can't you? It shouldn't be any problem for you—that is, if you *really* are the Son of God."

Jesus was ready. "It would be easier to create bread than not to. But I am God, *your* God. If I stoop and put myself under your authority, even this one time, mankind will have only bread forever. Satan, I will not let you take the Word of God out of their mouths by putting a piece of bread into mine."

So Jesus remained true. But there were other kinds of hunger; centuries of deception had proven it so to the tempter. "Wouldn't it be grand to receive all the comfort and adulation of your holy angels...right now? After all those days of loneliness in the wilderness? Look down from this wall. Can't you just envision your hosts rushing to your aid if you threw yourself down there? They wouldn't let the Son of God hit the ground. Or is that who you really are? You don't act much like the Son of God. You seem too weak even to help yourself; how are you going to help others?"

"It would give me no end of pleasure," Jesus replied, "to prove to you in an instant who I am. I would love to command my angels to rescue me. But I am God, and if I give in to your temptation to indulge myself, then mankind will follow your wicked example of tempting God. They won't know the security of having a God who doesn't compromise with evil. They won't have courage against your suggestions to jump from the pinnacle."

Again Jesus dodged temptation. But Satan wasn't finished. He came against Jesus at Jesus' point of deepest feeling. "I know how eager you are to establish your kingdom on earth. Look out from this mountaintop. Imagine all the kingdoms out there. Think of all the subjects you could have and all the glory they would give you! And you would deserve every bit of their worship. *I* don't want their worship. I'd be content with *your* worship alone. Think of it! All I'd have would be your worship, but you'd have the adoration of everyone else! You *do* deserve that, do you not?"

The Savior was angry. "In some ways it would be easy to fall down and worship you. Then I'd be rid of you! But you've forgotten once again that I am your God, and if I worship you, then mankind will have no choice but to do the same. All creation would have to serve you. And frankly, Satan, the very thought of my children on their knees before you is the most detestable thing I can imagine. I'm resisting you yet again so they might have courage to know that, in my strength, they can do the same."

The tempter consoled himself that there'd be other days and other places and other people.

Jesus knew the same. He closed his eyes, looked down through the centuries, and saw others. One was out in the wilderness. Another on a high wall. Still another on a mountaintop.

And he prayed for each one by name.

Matthew 4:1–11

FOR REFLECTION: Do I respond to temptation in ways that make Jesus glad he stood strong?

HE COULD HAVE CALLED TEN THOUSAND ANGELS

What would you think of a man who had the resources and the right to defend himself but who, deliberately and repeatedly, did not?

You'd likely categorize him as a weakling, am I right?

As an avowed people watcher, that was my immediate conclusion as well. I assumed I had encountered a classic coward.

But he caught my attention early on as a person who didn't fit the timid category on one simple yet crucial point: The external signs of cowardice were not accompanied by an internal lack of resolve. On the contrary, this man possessed the stamina and determination of a decathlete. His purposeful drive would have taken him to the top of any endeavor he might have chosen to pursue.

Why then the failure to stand up for his own rights?

Let me explain my conundrum more specifically.

He was, as far as I could determine, a man without a malicious bone in his body. I couldn't see any person he hated or wished evil upon.

Yet he experienced a more unfortunate string of bad luck than I would wish on my bill collector: One of his closest friends betrayed him while his other associates vanished into the woods. He was treated viciously by the authorities and was maligned and slandered by the sort who have no reputation for truthfulness.

Yet all the while, our man hardly said a word in his own defense.

Honestly, I couldn't imagine what he might have done to bring such abuse on himself. He must have committed some serious crime.

Perhaps the anomaly came into sharpest relief in the garden called Gethsemane. There it is said he prayed for deliverance from the whole ordeal that eventually befell him.

Any observer of even mediocre ability could surmise that this man faced an incredibly painful prospect. He seemed on the verge of fulfilling an unseen obligation, bearing an invisible weight.

I found myself wondering how important it could have been to endure such agony, especially if, as it appeared to me, he was doing so voluntarily. Wouldn't the people he owed understand his inability to make good on his promise? Wouldn't those who hoped in him recover from their disappointment?

Though I normally stay noncommittal as far as other people's problems are concerned, I inwardly wished he would quit. *Don't put yourself through any more of this. Have some self-respect. Give it up!*

What I was witnessing was a man battling with the most pivotal decision of his life. He stood on the brink, clearly having two choices.

I cannot explain the reason, but he took the harder road.

Why?

The answer seemed to lie, at least partially, in his relationship with his father. The son had such a strong sense of duty toward him. Was he paying his father's debt, I wondered.

Whatever the background, both were equally committed to going forward.

I'll admit that at first I thought the father must be very cruel to insist on his finishing. But the longer I studied their relationship, the more fully I became convinced that the father endured as much empathetic agony as his son. They shared something very deep. They both resisted the temptation to abandon their principles.

Finally, the ultimate happened, something I was sure would knock sense into the man: He was erroneously condemned to death. I thought surely this would force him to release the passion that drove him forward.

Surely this would be the final straw that would cause him to defend himself.

But the pitiable man held on to his inner pact. *Does he love sorrow?* He gritted his teeth and refused to give up.

Though all hell enticed him to quit (or so it seemed to me as an observer), though nothing and no one forced him to go forward, though he could have called for reinforcements from his father's staff, though he could have overcome his persecutors (for he was easily the better man than they), yet his face was set. He resisted even a sideways glance.

It will puzzle me to my grave. I fully expect that never in my lifetime will I meet another man who could—or for that matter would—choose such a course.

I believe he did what no one else has done or will do. And I'm baffled as to what sets him apart. All I can think of is that the poor fellow must have had some kind of a messiah complex.

Mark 14:32–36; Hebrews 12:2–3; 1 Peter 2:21–24

FOR REFLECTION: Do I make the harder, and better, choice for Christ as he did for me?

CHAPTER THIRTEEN

IMAGINE HIM SERVING YOU

To serve.

It's what the dictionary compilers define as "giving the service and respect due a superior; complying with the commands or demands of another."

It's what a person does when he

lends a helping hand,
ministers,
waits on hand and foot,
offers refreshments,
is at someone's beck and call,
waits on a table,
satisfies another's desires,
bows down, or
accommodates.

It's what the Son of God did, the one whom the Bible calls

Head and High Priest,
Potentate and Prince,
Captain and Commander,
King of Israel and King of kings,

Master and Mighty God,
Refiner and Rock,
Governor and Glory,
Lion of Judah and Lord of lords,
Jehovah and Judge.
It's what the Son of God had no need to do.

And there you have yet another of the great enigmas of Jesus. What he did had neither precedent nor comparison. It's neither comprehensible as to cost nor fathomable as to implication.

It can only be looked upon in wonder:

The Son of God served.

EXPOSED BY GREATNESS

"Suppose one of you had a servant plowing or looking after the sheep. Would he say to the servant when he comes in from the field, 'Come along now and sit down to eat'? Would he not rather say, 'Prepare my supper, get yourself ready and wait on me while I eat and drink; after that you may eat and drink'? Would he thank the servant because he did what he was told to do? So you also, when you have done everything you were told to do, should say, 'We are unworthy servants; we have only done our duty.'"—Jesus of Nazareth, as quoted in the ancient document, the Gospel according to Luke (17:7–10)

Servanthood and humility exemplify the same lack of self-awareness. In pure form, servanthood and humility think little of whether anyone notices them. They just delight to be. Wearing no pretense or expectation, they're naturally unassuming.

Pride on the other hand is gaudy and overdressed. Showy. That's why, when meeting true servanthood, pride feels conspicuous and out of place. Or should. Too often pride blunders forward, blinded to his own pomposity, ignorant of how inappropriate he appears in others' eyes.

That's what happened in a Jerusalem guest room the night before Christ died. The disciples had been showing off their best outfits, competing for the prize of recognition. Then they suddenly found themselves in the presence of a true servant, and they were caught with their proverbial pants down.

"I don't see any servant around here carrying water. This is a low income area; I don't think anyone living here can afford slaves."

Peter and John dispatched their duties grudgingly. Finally spotting their man ("You go talk to him, John"), Peter mused: *Why couldn't the Lord have asked Andrew to do this? I thought Jesus recognized my gift of leadership. My brother is better suited to errands and arrangements; he has done them all his life.*

John returned, trying in every way to be the peer. "Hope that servant doesn't go too far off with that water; we'll need him later."

Peter and John led the others into the room prepared for the feast, and the Twelve bickered among themselves over which of them was the greatest:

"Wait a minute, who got out of the boat and onto the water?"

"But not all are called 'Beloved.'"

"Only one of us was his first disciple, and you're looking at him."

"Peter wouldn't have met Christ if it hadn't been for me."

All twenty-six feet in the room that evening were dusty. The servant whose availability John had hoped for had not appeared. The time was ripe for washing; the meal was about to begin. Competitive emotions still lingered in the disciples, making humility a rare commodity. A water basin and a towel sat in the corner.

It was an opportunity for greatness.

An opportunity ignored.

Until the one person in the room who had the least cause to serve did just that.

"No, Lord, I won't let you wash my feet. Ever!"

The garish garb of pride was suddenly and embarrassingly exposed. All those who had contributed to the greatness debate were stung by the emergence of raw servanthood. Those who had held back from the competition (if any did) wrestled with the pride of false humility.

The water must have felt cool and soothing. The patting of the soft towel was surely a comfort.

But deep down it must have hurt. *Why didn't I get up and do it when I felt the inclination? Did I have to be so stubborn?*

Even to the end, the dearth of servanthood had ample illustration.

"I have given you an example to follow," he had said. Yet four historical records (two of which, John's and Matthew's, were eyewitness accounts) lead us to believe that having washed his disciples' feet, the Son of God

instituted the Lord's Supper,
gave his great discourse on the True Vine,
offered up his High Priestly prayer,
agonized in the garden,
endured betrayal and arrest,
and went to the cross,

all the while having feet that no one had even considered washing.

And perhaps even more remarkably, the Son of God probably thought nothing of it.

Luke 22:7–30; John 13:1–17

FOR REFLECTION: What forms do the basin and towel need to take in my life?

THE KING

There was a time, though not in time, when all the heads in heaven turned.

The scene was filled with the full regalia of the presence of Majesty. Twenty-four glorious thrones stood in a complete circle like faithful sentries. On each one sat an elder dressed in white and crowned with gold.

Their glorious appearance, contrary to expectation, drew one's attention past them and irresistibly toward the center. There, one found the unapproachably brilliant hub of the universe: the very throne of the Godhead.

Whose pen could describe the wonders to be seen there? The throne seemed to rise out of a sea of glass, as clear as crystal. Surrounding it were the holiest of angels, continually offering praise to the Triune God. Seven lamps blazed before the throne.

Above, a rainbow encircled the scene like a halo. Lightning flashed. And as if none of the senses should be ignored, peals of thunder joined in the celebration.

But the most beautiful part of the scene wasn't something one could measure in brightness or color.

Only in feeling. In commitment. In love.

All heaven knew that what made the throne room shimmer with beauty was Relationship. The Father and the Son, gripped eternally by oneness and closeness and partnership. Sharing together their rightful glory from before beginnings began.

The Father looked at his Son with pride. And well he should, for what he saw in his Son was Kingship from head to foot. Eyes blazing with righteous fire, feet like glowing bronze. His voice was like the sound of rushing waters, and out of his mouth came truth, as incisive as a double-edged sword. His head and hair glowed. And in his right hand he held seven stars.

He wore a crown and a robe. His chest bore a golden sash, his pose adorned by a kingly scepter.

Yes, the Father looked at him with pride, gazing as if to take one last look.

And then he nodded to his Son with a smile meant to reassure.

And in response, God the Son stood.

When the time was absolutely right, God the Son stood.

Only then did it happen. Only then did the world of the angels collide with the unexpected.

The Son of God took off his robe. Resolutely he set down his scepter. Removed his crown of glory and honor. Set aside the stars of grandeur.

Indeed, not until then did shock waves crash onto the farthest shores of eternity. It was not a thing of shame. It was just the holy indecency of the King of heaven taking off his glory.

How could it be? And for what senseless purpose?

Unbelievability had made its debut in the throne room.

And then Mary, Joseph, a few farm animals, and all of heaven heard a baby cry.

And the Father kept watching. And smiling approvingly.

He watched as his Son grew and learned and obeyed.

He watched as he recruited and trained and challenged.

Then one day the Father watched his Son walk up a hill by himself. The Father gazed on his Son with pride, and well he should, for what he saw in his Son was Humiliation from head to foot.

The blaze now gone from his eyes, they held the look of brokenness and compassion. His feet were pierced to bring peace.

His voice was stilled, sheathed till another time. His head and hair were matted in sweaty blood.

He wore a crown of piercing mockery. His robe was once again removed but now as a gambler's bounty. His chest bore the blow from an impatient guard. His pose impressed no one.

His hands were empty.

The rainbow had turned to darkness, the throne now a cross rising out of a sea of scorn and hate.

And as for standing, the King couldn't.

But do you know? There was still beauty that day. Not the kind which can be measured in brightness or color.

Only in feeling. In commitment. In love.

By now all heaven knew that what made Humiliation beautiful was Relationship. The Father and the Son, gripped eternally by oneness and closeness and partnership.

That's why the Father looked at his Son approvingly. He gazed upon him, as if to take one last look. He nodded to his Son with a smile meant to reassure.

And then he had to look away.

Philippians 2:5–8; Revelation 4:1–6; 1:12–16

FOR REFLECTION: Do I seek the beauty of humility?

FEAST IN THREE COURSES

It had been a long and lonely night. For more than our four-hour shift, we had borne the pain of hunger, discouragement, and disillusionment.

As the early sun edged its way over the black ridge of hills surrounding the lake, our hunger pains stabbed deeper because we hadn't caught anything to eat the whole night. Nothing.

It was then we heard the shout of a familiar voice coming from the nearby shore. Someone, we couldn't tell who, inquired about the success of our attempt. *Probably another fisherman scouting areas where the fish are running this morning.* Perhaps out of a last-ditch hope, we followed the stranger's advice to try the other side of the boat.

You know the rest.

Suddenly we heard a splash, and Peter was in the water! The rest of us followed and found on the beach the very thing we craved: a warm breakfast. The Master had already started the fire and was cooking fresh fish for us all. He had us sit down, and he served us right there on the beach that we all knew and loved so well.

Jesus knew that it wasn't just our stomachs that were hungering. Our confidence needed bolstering. That's why that morning will always linger in our memories.

As we sat there eating, our conversation turned to the first time the Lord's insight had brought us a huge catch. We laughed at how we had first protested against trying again after a whole night of fruitless labor.

Having the Lord do it again, when we least expected it, reminded us that he was still the same Master with the same power, even now. He fed us a generous helping of assurance that we were still fishers of men. Nothing had changed.

Jesus wanted to make yet one more contribution to our troubled band. Our spokesman was still stinging from the pain of the three denials he had made. And we all knew it.

And so the Lord seemed to have a meal of restoration in mind. He served it up with eloquence. "Simon, do you love me more than these?"

We all knew that Peter had stood in the courtyard of the high priest. We knew he had said he wasn't one of Jesus' disciples. The words, burning in his memory, were still too painful to confess.

Which Jesus realized.

Is that why he tenderly and skillfully reaffirmed Peter with the dignity of an important task?

"Feed my lambs."

A few days had not erased the story (perhaps years would never do so) of how Peter, as he warmed himself by the fire alongside the servants and officials of the courtyard, had said he didn't know or understand anything about the Nazarene.

How gracious of the Lord, we thought, for him to reiterate to Peter, "Take care of my sheep." It was as if he was saying, "Failure doesn't disqualify."

In the Master's wisdom, his assurance to Peter was not yet full. For each cursing he gave a blessing.

Simon had sworn, "I don't even know the man!" And so Jesus for the third time blessed him with full restoration. "Feed my sheep."

At that moment the tension was high. What would Peter say? What would Jesus say?

For a moment no one said anything.

Then unexpectedly a rooster crowed. And beginning with a grin from Jesus, followed by the same from Peter, we all started to laugh a laugh that built up and eventually erupted into full-bellied guffaws!

Jesus had served up a feast to remember.

John 18:15–27; 21:1–17;

FOR REFLECTION: What are my hunger pains that the Master wants to satisfy?

CHAPTER FOURTEEN

IMAGINE HIM FORGIVING YOU

You couldn't have been any farther east. You were burdened with an indefinable weight, unable to analyze it or get a grip on it or rid yourself of it. And no one could help you with it.

Until a man came and, taking your burden as if it weighed hardly anything, carried it up and across a range of mountains.

On his climb, a seductive woman, a woman called Justice, intercepted him. She reasoned with him, saying, "The one whose burden you carry doesn't deserve your efforts. Lay down the weight, and stop your journey in the name of fairness."

Your man kept going.

By and by he passed through a desert, traversing its barrenness for days on end. Under the scorching sun, a strapping young man called Reality approached him. "You're carrying that heavy weight for someone who won't even appreciate what you're doing. Not only that, he won't always relieve others of their burdens, even when given the chance. Let me take care of it for you right now. You won't have to carry it any farther."

Acknowledging the young man, your burden bearer nevertheless persevered. Soon he came upon a deep forest, so thick that sunlight could scarcely penetrate it. An old man with many years of experience in the world met up with him. The graybeard was called Restitution. "You," said the elderly man, "with that burden on your back. I see that you're very determined, since you have made it this far. But realizing all the work this requires of you, you must go to the owner of this burden and make him pay for the relief you have provided."

But the burden bearer passed through the forest without stopping.

Soon he came to the end of his journey. He had gone as far west as he possibly could. There he faced the deepest of oceans.

He removed your burden and threw it into the heart of that sea, where to this day it is still sinking.

CAUGHT IN THE ACT

Mine was not an elaborate plan. Her lover was my neighbor. I knew the times they met. And the current place.

This was useful information for a young scribe trying to get some recognition, trying to get the nod for advancement among the ranks. Exposing a sinner was the heady stuff that promotions were made of. Especially if one could catch the transgressor in the very act. Such a juicy morsel made our men of God drool.

I let two of my friends in on the plan. We caught them. Brought her in. The mouths of the elders watered as if on cue. "Teacher, this woman was caught in the act of adultery. In the Law, Moses commanded us to stone such women. Now what do you say?"

The Teacher bent down and scratched in the soil with a stick, appearing to ignore us. Then he spoke. I heard his words, but it was his meaning that sank in: Adultery was only one kind of sin. It was the kind our victim had committed. The ones we had committed simply had different names.

I heard the ammunition of my accomplices drop randomly to the ground. Slowly at first. Then like an avalanche.

A war raged within me. My pride fought off conviction till my last ounce of strength had expired. Finally I let go.

I was the last to drop my stones of hate, for I was the last to admit that I too had been caught in the very act.

Turning, I walked away and melted into the crowd. I lingered and watched Jesus with the woman I had trapped. Ironically I envied her. She at least knew where she stood. She knew what she was. She had nowhere to look but up.

I, on the other hand, still had my respectability. My pride. My external competence wrestling the emptiness within.

Later, after the street had cleared of spectators, I returned to the very spot where I had thrown the woman to the ground. My eyes were drawn to the place nearby where Jesus had written in the dirt. It was still readable enough. He had written her name, at least originally. He had then drawn a cross through her name, and on the side he had written *charis,* grace.

A rush of blood went to my head. My knees felt weak. I pictured myself plotting to catch her in sin, admitting to myself that it had somehow gratified my own lust. I remembered my selfish zeal and my hatred as I readied myself to throw stones at her.

Kneeling now, I realized that she and I were just the same, equally in need of forgiveness. I reached out, and under the word *grace* I wrote my own name.

I guess it was my way of apologizing. My way of saying I would never, ever, do it again. The words I had overheard rang in my mind, and I somehow knew they were also true for me: "Go and sin no more."

I rose, a free man.

John 8:1–11

FOR REFLECTION: Am I aware of my pervasive use of self-justification? Am I truly sick of it yet?

DOUBLE PARALYSIS

Paralysis—a state of powerlessness or incapacity to act

Jesus always gets energized when he sees faith. In fact, outlandish faith seems to bring on his outlandish power.

Such was the experience one day when, as Jesus was teaching in a house, a commotion was heard on the roof. Soon, rays of light poked into the room as clay tiles were lifted away one by one. Jesus lost the attention of his crowd as a bent human form descended through the opening.

Jesus smiled approvingly at the bundle of faith before him. He instantly diagnosed the disease: double paralysis.

Like any good physician, Jesus dealt with the more serious ailment first: "Son, your sins are forgiven."

The skeptics in the crowd immediately challenged his right to say such a thing. They accused him of fooling the people, for they saw no proof backing up his words.

Jesus asked them: "Is it easier to transform a life or to transform an eternity?"

The doubters doubted.

The crowd marveled.

The paralytic sensed that his faith was about to be stretched.

Jesus went on: "If I heal his legs, everyone will see it, and the crowd will cheer. But if I heal his spirit, only he will know, while all heaven rejoices.

"One disease requires the mending of nerves and muscles, the strengthening of bones and fibers. The other demands the condescension of God to earth, the shaming of the shameless Son of God.

"Even restored legs will eventually grow old, but a forgiven life will never even wrinkle."

The skeptics accused him of trickery, sly talk.

The man with twisted legs looked up through the hole at his friends. He needed no proof. The certainty of the easier was outweighed by the hope of the harder.

I thought I wanted to walk out of this house without pain. But now I realize I want to walk into heaven without condemnation.

Graciously Jesus gave him both.

Everybody eventually left that house that day. But many of them were now on another journey.

Mark 2:1–12

FOR REFLECTION: Am I enamored with the kind of healing that cost Jesus more?

OVATION

In some ways I wish I could have met him earlier in life and under better circumstances. If only I could have had some dignity or wealth to offer him. If only I had had time to prove my gratitude for what he did for me or to tell others about him.

But in another way I wouldn't change a thing. At least not the ending.

Forgive me for being obtuse. May I back up and tell you a bit of my story?

Growing up I always loved the arts though I had very little success on the stage. In fact, no success. But in private I was a master, if you know what I mean. As a lad and even into young manhood I used to act out my favorite scenes from great plays when no one else was around.

I suppose I came by all of this naturally, because my parents lived for the theater. They were both married to the stage, and the offspring of their hearts were the actors and actresses they discovered and trained.

It didn't take me long to figure out that, due to my lack of promise, I would have to find my own role in the drama. Creating make-believe intrigue backstage, I sneaked around like a sly rat, amusing myself with mischief and trickery. I would get attention for myself by aggravating others and by snatching trinkets and money from unsuspecting pockets.

I'm afraid the rest of the tale unfolds as an uninteresting string of failures, rejected attempts at one thing and the other. Respectability eluded me. Trouble didn't. And eventually everything unraveled for me when I got caught red-handed.

Then I found myself on the way of the cross, the path everyone dreaded. (When it became obvious to me that I was to suffer crucifixion, I found my mind musing over the irony of it all. You see, my father had directed a play called "The Skull." It was an intense drama. Highly acclaimed. The play got its name from the climax when Lucifer, the villain, had his skull crushed in defeat. His conqueror, wounded but triumphant, went straight to the prison, broke open the gates as if they had no lock, and released all the captives. That final scene always used to bring the house down.)

Much of that entire day remains unclear in my thinking. I was so tired.

But I can't forget watching the hammer come down and wincing my eyes closed and feeling the shock waves of pain come through the bone all the way up to my shoulder.

I saw him wince, too.

I remember when they lifted up my cross and poised it vertically over the hole in the ground and thrust it recklessly against the bottom; I remember feeling the pull of my flesh and screaming out when my hands and feet felt as if they would tear off.

I heard him scream, too.

Indeed, I'll never forget being crucified with Christ.

Never forget the honor. Something had finally gone my way: scheduled by fate to die alongside a famous man.

The third member of our "party" had a different view. He was just as abusive as the crowds along the way. Just as vulgar as the guards.

I put the fool in his place. *Finally, my soliloquy! Odd stage perhaps, and an audience of but one. But it was something at least.*

"Don't you fear God since you are under the same sentence? We are punished justly, for we are getting what our deeds deserve. But this man has done nothing wrong."

Where did that come from? Was that me? Indeed, he is *different. Not just because of his notoriety. Look at the way he's taking all of this. I believe he's the*

Messiah. "Jesus, remember me when you come into your kingdom."

At the time I honestly didn't know if his reply was real or a result of my delirium. But what a joy I felt! (Imagine being a dozen heartbeats from death, stripped of all decency and decorum, and receiving eternal life!)

Before long, darkness descended like a cloudy scrim. But I was feeling the strangest light from inside.

Today...

I knew I was nearly naked, but do you know, I felt fully robed.

Together...

I knew I had been beaten, but I wasn't despairing at all. Struck down but not destroyed.

Paradise.

My life started as it ended. Glory came from shame, acceptance from accusation.

For just before the final curtain, the Victor opened the prison door. And my, you should have heard the angels cheer!

Luke 23:39–43

FOR REFLECTION: Do I appreciate the awesome privilege of being crucified with Christ? Do I realize that I was?

CHAPTER FIFTEEN

IMAGINE HIM SUFFERING FOR YOU

Did you ever stop to consider that God never had to *obey* anyone? The concepts of deity and obedience are mutually exclusive. God rules. His *subjects* obey.

Not only that, God never had to *learn* anything either. Forever he has known everything there is to know. Learning suggests a need to gain something. It suggests a lack of information or of proficiency. God has never had and will never have such a lack.

That's why Jesus is such an anomaly. He's an enigma on both counts, for the Bible says that "Although he was a son, he learned obedience..." (Hebrews 5:8).

The eternal Logos, who brought all knowledge into being, deliberately took a position among his creation so that he would have to *learn*—something he didn't need to do. And what he learned was *obedience*—something he didn't need to know!

Perhaps even more shocking is the way he learned. The verse finishes, "Although he was a son, he learned obedience *from what he suffered.*" The all-knowing Son of God didn't need to learn what obedience was or how one did it. Then why did he endure it? Perhaps he volunteered so he could learn *what it cost a human to obey.* And the only way to do that was to be mentored by the teacher called Suffering.

In hours of gut-wrenching prayer in a garden, in Jerusalem's halls of injustice, on the executioner's cruel hill, Suffering taught Jesus the cost of obedience.

But leave behind for a moment these incidents when Suffering instructed Christ. Look with me beyond the level of his physical pain and the injustice of the treatment he received. Is there not even more wonder in the suffering of Jesus Christ?

Does not your heart ache when you consider that the man being mocked was actually the Logos who never needed to learn anything? Does it not take you aback to remember that the ribs and flesh they whipped belonged to the only true God who never had to obey anyone?

For the eternal God-man to grit his teeth and intentionally endure suffering so he could bring his creation back to himself and spare them from eternal damnation in hell, and for him to endure alienation from his Father in the process...well, the very idea must have been sheer torture.

A FRIEND'S KNIFE CUTS DEEPEST

I followed at a distance as I often did. It was not my place to be noticed. Not usually.

He had often retreated with his disciples to the grove of trees called Gethsemane. I had accompanied them there before. I had heard his lessons there. Had witnessed his teaching them truths they'd need to know.

I knew he was preparing them to labor for his kingdom, but winds of trouble whistled through the branches that night. The stench of a traitor was unmistakable.

Perhaps the very idea of betrayal involves shock. It requires being surprised by the disloyalty of one trusted. Otherwise it would be the predictable assault of open warfare. For that reason it seems betrayal wounds more deeply.

I watched as the conspiracy gathered momentum. Eyes glaring and staring like torches piercing the night. Furtive glances. Nervous laughter. And before long the spears appeared, weapons of intimidation. Swords were unsheathed that they might threaten and scare. Why were they there?

The captors' blood thirst had been triggered by the scent of a betrayer, their appetite for excitement whetted by the drama of one willing to stab his friend in the back.

Who was this betrayer, this "friend"? One chosen for friendship. One who owed much more than he gave. But for the shortsighted lust of thirty pieces of fleeting status, thirty rotting bits of revenge, or thirty moments in an ephemeral spotlight, one who unashamedly sold out a faithful companion to strangers.

The manner of his betrayal was equally true to form. He feigned faithfulness. Shielded behind a cloak of familiarity, he carried a dagger till the moment of untruth. Suddenly it was unsheathed, and the deed, meant to appear so innocent and even affectionate, was done with deadly intent.

The other onlookers were as stunned as I.

A true friend who was present wanted to stop it all but didn't know how. Finally, in near desperation, he lashed out recklessly and without skill, his intent noble, his effect clumsy. He did not see the bigger picture as Jesus did.

Also present was one conspirator by default. Malchus was there, not out of any conviction of his own but because others expected him to be. He'd rather have been home reading a book (and should have been). But there he was, an innocent accomplice to another's hate and paying dearly for it.

I watched and wondered: *Is there anything so brutal as being stabbed by a friendly knife?*

And then I saw the answer. Worse yet was to be so stabbed and have even your true friends abandon you, to watch shame and confusion sever the cords of commitment.

He had told the Father with such pride, "I have not lost one of those you gave me." Yet there he stood, completely alone.

In my bitterness at the vanity of their promises and my disappointment at the shallowness of their discipleship, I was tempted to say to him that you cannot lose what never existed.

But I didn't.

I couldn't. Could not say a word.

He was the Son of the Most High. He would sit forever on the throne of his father David.

To see him now, friendless and abandoned, jerked by the clutches of enemies, was beyond credibility. *How can men treat their God thus? Do they not know who is among them? Show them your glory, O Son. Let them see even a portion of the brilliance I have seen in you.*

I wanted to call out. But it was not for me to speak.

And then they came after me, like animals in the wild, feeding with frenzy. I had seen stupidity incarnate in the mob of men.

Mark 14:43–52; John 18:1–11; Luke 1:31–32

FOR REFLECTION: How can I handle betrayal as Jesus did? How can I ensure that I will never wield the blade?

THE TRAP

It must have been a tremendous comfort to the people living in those days to know they could depend on the unflagging efforts of so many caretakers of justice.

On the Jewish side, the Sadducees and the Pharisees united in the high court of the people called the Sanhedrin, the judicial council consisting of the best minds with the best pedigree in Israel. Leading this august group was their president, the high priest, perceived as the most holy man in the nation.

On the Roman side stood the brilliant administrator Pontius Pilate. His crosstown cohort was Herod the Tetrarch, the Jews' unwanted king and the Romans' handy pawn.

With so many committed to fair rule, the streets themselves should have flowed with justice.

But such was not the case. Hatred and envy divided these judicial minds. The Sadducees hated the Pharisees, making the high court an ongoing theological tug-of-war. Pilate despised Herod; their co-location in Jerusalem only served to heighten awareness of their political competitiveness. And if that was not enough, the Jews hated the Romans—the ruled despising the rulers.

The unpeaceful nature of their coexistence grew year by year. Mutual spite echoed through their chambers and corridors. They viewed one another with the kind of affection shared by a pack of snarling dogs.

Until one day a lamb walked among them.

Simultaneously their eyes lit up. Simultaneously they rubbed their hands together in hungry anticipation. Simultaneously they dug a pit, stretched a net over it, and camouflaged it.

The lamb saw the trap, recognized it as his destiny, and walked calmly and quietly toward it.

Meanwhile, the guardians of purity fumbled all over themselves to ensure that the lamb went where he intended to go anyway.

Can you fathom the absurdity of a high priest—the pride and joy of Jewishness, the mediator between God and a people needing pardon—floundering in a clumsy effort to snag the very Lamb of God in a net of trumped-up charges and false witnesses?

Picture it. With access to two milleniums of wisdom from God's Word and God's prophets, the chosen leaders of God's chosen people offered insightful statements such as...

> Release, for the blessing of our people, the rebel and robber and murderer, instead of the teacher and healer and miracle worker.
>
> We wouldn't deign to step into the court of Pilate lest we be ceremonially defiled, but we have no king but Caesar.
>
> Whatever you say, Pilate. Consider yourself innocent of the blood of this lamb, and (to show that prophecy was not yet dead) may his blood be on us and on our children.

Pontius Pilate learned quickly. So intently did he wish to see justice done at any political price that this jewel of wisdom fell from his lips: I find no fault in him, so take him out and kill him yourselves.

It was a showcase of justice miscarried, protocol ignored, and a hidden agenda that could not have been more obvious. Justice never crossed anyone's mind.

And so in the end, with eyes wide open the lamb stepped into the net.

Malicious witnesses rise up against me. I stumble, and they rejoice. They gather themselves together; smiters gather together. They slander without ceasing.

Like godless jesters at a feast they gnash at me with their teeth. They wink at one another. Devising deceitful words, they open their mouths wide, saying, "Aha, aha, our eyes have seen it!"

Tangled, the lamb was silent.

How long will you look on, Father? Rescue my soul from their ravages, my only life from the lions. Do not let those who are wrongfully my enemies rejoice over me. You have seen it, O Lord. Do not keep silent. O Lord, do not be far from me. Stir up thyself, and awake to my right and to my cause.

But it was his lot to endure injustice.

And so it was, with their catch secured at the bottom of the pit, that the bitterest of enemies—the Sadducees and Pharisees, Pilate and Herod, the Jews and the Romans—all gathered and shook unholy hands on a job well done.

Matthew 26:57–27:26; Psalm 35:7–23; Isaiah 53:7–8

FOR REFLECTION: When I cry out in frustration at injustices perpetrated against me, do I hear his still, small voice whisper, "I understand"?

MAN OF SORROWS

I would be the talk of the jailhouse *this* time.

My first arrest was for assault, the second for insurrection (when I was moving around with Barabbas). Then it was assault with intent to kill.

Serious enough, but now I really had their attention: murder.

Or did I? I was in for only a few hours when I realized I was being upstaged. Something even bigger than murder was in the offing, so they placed me in a holding cell to wait my turn.

At least my cell was a good vantage point for viewing the action.

Now, I'm no one to talk, but those who handle prisoners indulge themselves in unnecessary violence. Every time they've hauled me into these halls I've wondered what the difference is between the prisoners and the majority of the guards. Why is their assault legal and mine not?

It was on the stage of such legal and gratuitous cruelty that I saw the one who was stealing the attention I should have received. His cry of agony was the first I saw or heard of him. I looked down the corridor and saw the guards leading him to Pilate.

He was on all fours, trying to recover. A thug in uniform stood over him with a club secured by both hands, waiting for his next urge to demonstrate his intelligence.

I assumed by that time in the proceedings the accused had received his fair share of face slapping and vulgarity. A cellmate confirmed my suspicion. In fact, he added that this Jesus was at odds with the religious establishment as well and had been worked over by them the whole night. Apparently they had played quite a game with him, covering his face with a sack, then taking turns beating him and saying, "Prophesy. Who hit you?" As I said, something happens to these vermin when they get fresh meat.

There was now some commotion in the hall: It was time for this man's scourging. Though I did not care at all for this captured lout, I winced internally, for I knew from personal experience the hell he was about to endure. The boot of a soldier put him to the floor over the whipping block. (I found myself reaching unconsciously to feel the ribs on my right side. Several of them had been fractured when I got my scourging, limiting me to half-breaths for months.) The rough balls of lead fixed to the ends of leather straps accelerated into his back. I watched numbly. Dozens of lashes. Someone remarked on how silent he was.

I figured that would be the end of it. Scourging normally was the climax of vileness. But the soldiers were in unusual form that day. The whole cohort seemed to have gathered for a show.

Someone stripped off the rag Jesus still wore, pulling bits of shredded skin from his back. Another produced a purple robe and covered the open wounds in mocking pomp. With the same laughing ridicule, still another came forward with a crude stick to serve as a scepter. And then came the final touch that all were waiting for: a crown woven from a long thorn branch. They spiked it into his flesh to a loud cheer of derision.

And then to complete their pageant, the whole cohort began bowing in a spoof on worship. Their jeering voices filled the corridor all the way down to my cell: "Hail, King of the Jews! Hail, King of the Jews!"

After this sport had run its course, Jesus disappeared from my view. But again my location allowed me to hear everything that happened. There was a tremendous cheer from a large crowd that had gathered outside the Praetorium. A voice tried, then finally succeeded, quieting them down. Then an announcement: "Behold the man!"

The throng erupted in chanting, "Kill the wretch! Crucify him! Nail him up!"

I thought I had seen the last of him at that point, but only because I had forgotten that those sentenced to death are brought through the very corridor along which I was stationed. *What luck! I'll get to see him up close. Maybe I'll spit on him, too.*

As he approached, my cellmates went into action. It was a normal reaction to jeer and spit and try to hit the condemned. Don't ask me why.

We were all shouting. When he passed me, I yelled out, "You! Fake king! What are you in for?"

I was startled when he stopped, just for an instant before a guard jerked him forward again, just long enough for him to answer, "I'm in for you."

Strange thing to say. Must be losing his mind.

Out toward Golgotha he went. All I could see was the purple robe.

I had forgotten to spit.

Matthew 26:57–68; 27:26–31; Isaiah 53:2–6

FOR REFLECTION: What difference does it make to me that Jesus was acquainted with grief?

CHAPTER SIXTEEN

IMAGINE HIM DYING FOR YOU

The Father beamed with pride. "Come to the table," he said, motioning as if before him lay a lavish feast of every kind of delicacy earth and heaven could offer. I expected there surely must be every kind of sweetmeat and every kind of tasty treat.

The table was big enough, to be sure. In fact, the table had room for anyone who wanted to sit. Room for anyone with an appetite.

But it wasn't full of food.

Only one bread cake.

And a single cup of wine.

Any disappointment I felt was immediately smothered by the effusive joy written all over the Father's face.

After I sat, he took the bread, and when he had blessed it, he broke it and gave me a piece. "Take, eat. This is the body of my beloved Son."

It wasn't a big piece, but it filled me up.

Then he took the cup, and when he had voiced his thanks, he handed it to me. "This is his blood of the covenant, which is shed for many."

I drank some of the wine. It was bitter but satisfying in every way.

The Father beams with pride.

"Come to the table," he says.

A HELLISH DILEMMA

Unbeknownst to earthlings, a massive problem was unfolding in the invisible creation. Only better minds than ours could grasp the immensity of the stakes, and only eternity will unveil the ingenuity, and the cost, of the solution.

First, there was the one true God, perfect in holiness. He desired fellowship with his human creation. It had to be a fellowship of holiness, for God was unwilling, indeed unable, to join with anything or anyone unholy.

Hence the problem. Having chosen as a race to rebel against God, humankind had become thoroughly infected with the unholy nature of our forefathers. Fellowship with our Creator was impossible.

What was the prospect of working out a solution to this dilemma?

We could not negotiate a compromise. Such an agreement would require each side to have something of value to offer the other party. In this case, God was the only one who had anything to offer.

So it was up to God. Only he could create a solution.

Or could he? His character bound him to a code of justice. He could not compromise his holiness by taking us as we were. Unholy cannot mix with holy.

Perhaps God's best option was to ignore us, to live without our fellowship. This was possible but, thankfully, not desirable on his part.

And so humankind had no option but to wait and hope. Only God had the power to devise a plan that could bring back to himself a sinful creation without compromising his hatred for sin.

It came down to only one possible solution. It was a stroke of genius, but it also meant maximum pain in God's heart.

He would punish sin. He would exact the necessary penalty of eternal death, thus preserving justice, winning forgiveness for humankind, and qualifying us for eternal life.

But at what cost? He could not apply the punishment on creation as we all deserved, for then no one would remain. All would perish in hell.

No, the sin of humankind would have to be fully punished in another way: God would have to let go of his Son. He'd have to give up his own to win back the rebels.

The "why?" of this solution is unfathomable. Eternity will hopefully explain it. But the "how?" is within our grasp, though barely. God the Father brought about his plan through a spiritual transaction of unimaginable proportions and eternal scope. To put it bluntly, God placed on his sinless Son all the sin of all humankind for all time—all at once—and punished his Son for all of it.

God took centuries to illustrate this solution to the world so that we could understand it. Each year on Yom Kippur (the Jewish Day of Atonement) the Israelite priest would take two goats. He'd kill the first goat to cover the people for their sin. The second one, the scapegoat, he'd send into the wilderness after symbolically placing all the Israelites' sin upon it.

When it came time for the real thing, the Son of God performed both functions, not symbolically but literally.

Like the high priest of old, God the Father placed on his Son the shame of every rape ever committed, the guilt of every murder, the filth of all vulgarity, the disgrace of all pride, lust, immorality, and abuse. Christ carried it all: every sinful nature of every man or woman, every sinful act ever committed, every mixed motive, every innuendo.

In a way that only God knows and only he could perform, he purposefully and thoughtfully placed every sin for all time—past, present, and future—on Christ's account. Christ became sin and suffered the penalty for it.

Unthinkable? Absolutely.

Impossible? Apparently not.

He was detestable. Despicable. No beauty. No majesty.

Sinfully ugly.

He was crushed under the weight of what you and I have done. What we *are* was upon him. Your sin made him unholy. And the Father had to separate himself.

That was the true torment of the crucifixion. The eternal bond between Father and Son had to be broken: "My God, My God, why have you forsaken me?"

How long would the Scapegoat have to bear sin? Wouldn't it depend on the seriousness of the sin he carried?

If our sinfulness required the penalty of eternal death, and if one person would normally be required to bear the sin of just one other, wouldn't Jesus be able to save only one human being?

And if that was so, wouldn't God's plan disappoint both him and us? Wouldn't it take billions of saviors to rescue billions of lost lives? Wouldn't an eternal debt take an eternity to pay?

Yes.

Unless...

Unless an eternal and infinite person could be that one life that would die for another. If that one person would be willing, he could bear an infinite amount of sin. He could pay an eternity of debt in a relative sliver of time. One such life would more than suffice to cover us all.

One such life did.

The Father couldn't bear to watch his beloved Son do this, but this is what happened. After placing all sin on his Son, the Father removed his hands. The Sin Bearer on the cross carried all sin into the wilderness, and when eternity and infinity were satisfied, he cried out with a loud voice, "It is finished!"

And that's all the Father needed to hear.

Leviticus 16:8–10, 20–22; Isaiah 53:1–12; John 3:16; 2 Corinthians 5:21
FOR REFLECTION: Have I felt the wonder that Christ bore every one of my sins, omitting nothing? That in Jesus Christ I do not stand condemned for even one thing?

ONCE A CROSS FELL DOWN

Stepping onto the ship moored in Mediterranean waters took my thoughts back three years to the day I met him. Not that we got acquainted near the water, but I had been coming to this ship to make this journey homeward when I was unexpectedly and unhappily delayed in Jerusalem.

I had stayed in the city only long enough to collect a few supplies. Though it was a melting pot of nations, I never felt comfortable in this place so unlike the deserts of my African homeland. Not to mention the crowded chaos that one could not escape even for a day.

Which brings me back to my story. I was walking a street which led out of town (because that's exactly where I wanted to go). I had stopped inside a small shop when I began hearing a loud commotion outside. Having paid for my provisions, I stepped into the doorway out of curiosity—a mistake. Passing by was a procession of those condemned to crucifixion. *Poor wretches! But nothing to do with me. Just move along and let me get on my way.*

The delay was a minor irritant; what followed was intolerable bad luck. One of the criminals staggered and fell right in front of the shop where I stood watching. A guard's spear pointed me out, and another's vicelike grip clutched my shirt and propelled me toward the cursed man on the pavement to help carry his cross.

Why me? Let someone else help him. I'm just an observer, and that's the way I like it.

I won't forget the sensation. The cross was heavier than I expected. And some people mistook me for the criminal on his way to die, even cursing me as I passed. *Curses on you! Don't you know this cross isn't mine?* And I remember thinking about the belongings I had left sitting on the floor of the shop (which I never got back).

Finally I reached the place where death was planned, and I threw the burdensome weapon of torment onto the ground, glad it wasn't intended for me. Freed of my obligation, I sought the anonymity of the crowd. I moved about, wanting to shed any association with the condemned.

Yet, don't ask me why, I stayed and watched.

He died differently than I had expected. Through eyes of resentment I saw in him a look of willingness.

The deed done, I went in search of my things. The shop owner feigned ignorance, and I knew I would now be held up for weeks until I could earn enough to replace my stolen supplies.

Held for a higher purpose.

Sometimes surprise begins in the subconscious. Then, as if on a short fuse, it ignites in conscious alarm. Such was my experience sometime later as I walked the same clinging alleyways: I heard a man preaching in my native language! Here in a hostile city I heard the words of my childhood and of my boyhood friends.

Like warm oil on brittle skin, their familiarity softened my defensiveness. They spoke of one who had died in the city not long before. One who died out of love, willingly.

It hit me with the force of a gale wind. Conviction and agony and remorse roared through my soul: It was he; the man who died was *my* criminal. I had helped crucify the Son of God. I had been all wrong; it *was* my cross I had carried!

How was I supposed to recognize you, Jesus? You were so weak you couldn't carry a wooden cross. How could I have known you were strong enough to bear the sins of the whole world?

I wanted to go back, to stand in the doorway of that shop once again, to hear the shouting of the crowd, to watch my Savior fall to the ground.

How I wanted to go back so I could jump unashamedly from among the bystanders, muster all my strength, and lift the cross from his bleeding back. To pick him up and help him along with my other arm. And to somehow find a few words that would encourage him along the way, some words to thank him for what he was doing for me. For me!

But of course the crowd had long since passed, and I was left with what I wished I had done.

Or was I? The message in my native tongue said he had to die. He had intended to do it all along. He did it to forgive.

To forgive even one who had a chance to show you kindness and didn't, even one who despised your cross, even one who missed his big chance?

As I resume my journey after these many months, I can say that the answer is yes. My heaviness has been taken away. I have left my regrets and shortcomings up on that hill.

But there's more good news. What I lost is being restored. The Savior has given me another chance to carry his cross…every day. It's still heavy, but it's the greatest privilege I know. Now I recognize a golden opportunity when I see one.

Mark 15:20–21; Acts 2:5–13, 22–24; Matthew 16:24–26

FOR REFLECTION: Do I perceive and appreciate the privilege of standing out from the crowd and bearing his cross?

THE SALVATION SYMPHONY

The prelude to Jesus Christ's death consisted of a gradual crescendo of spiritual frustration. Four realms felt the pressure.

One was embodied in a large and imposing structure in Jerusalem: the temple. An architectural masterpiece, the pearl of Herod also symbolized for the people a door—a closed door. To all Israel it represented the secrecy and holiness and remoteness of their God. To be in the Lord's presence was something they experienced vicariously, for God dwelt in the holy of holies behind the great veil. Centuries of separation from God had built up within the people, and they had no release from the pressure, for the veil which hid his presence was impenetrable. God dwelt in holy seclusion, an impersonal mystery.

Then there was the pressure building against the gates of Sheol. The just men and women of centuries gone by longed for their release into paradise.

The third point of tension was the separation of two peoples by a large and daunting wall. The have-nots looked longingly over the wall at those within. The former had been warded off for centuries, kept just out of reach of the promises, the hope, and the God of the privileged few who sat on the blessed side of the wall. Seemingly the hostility embodied by the imposing divider heightened year by year.

As if those days were not weighed down heavily enough, yet a fourth burden continued to oppress. It was nothing of great size, but its weight broke the backs of many a spirit. It was a certificate of debt. On the surface the decrees contained therein had every appearance of wise religiosity: "Do not handle; do not taste; do not touch." But these conscriptions were hostile to the soul's health. They had successfully ground all spiritual momentum to a halt.

And so it was that on the day Jesus died the world was crying out for release. Not knowing how or perhaps even why, the people of planet Earth needed God's deliverance.

And in just the moment of moments, God responded.

Hush now and listen, for the sounds of rescue are heard only by the trained ear. Listen for the symphony of salvation.

Unlike any other philharmonic, the concert you are about to hear has a ruggedness about it. It's even a bit crude. Yet to those who hear beyond the audible, it's unparalleled in beauty.

Place yourself on a lonely hill outside Jerusalem. The unlikely down-beat is the bleeding head of the Messiah slumping forward and bobbing briefly before becoming completely motionless. The cue is the death of the Son of God.

Listen now. Do you hear it? Off in the distance, do you hear that rumble? Do you hear that groaning in the quaking ground?

Isn't it the sound of tombs opening to the knock of a caller? Hear those locks turning. Hear those doors flinging wide! Hear those shouts, those laughs, those sounds of freedom!

Now add in the syncopation. Get the rhythm? Somebody's banging on a nail. Listen to the steadiness of that hand. Somebody means it. Somebody's angry.

Do you know what you're hearing? That's somebody nailing the certificate of debt to that cross. Somebody's doing away with all those decrees. Somebody's setting us free!

Crash! That's no cymbal. Crash! That's not a drum. Something just came down, came down for good. Sounded like a wall. The dust is clearing. Yes, it was a wall, the wall of enmity. I hear singing. I hear crying. I hear reconciling!

Now the symphony relaxes into pianissimo. Not a final hush, but one that tells you to keep attuned. What will we hear? A final chord? A frenetic refrain?

No, it's the unmistakable tearing of a curtain. A huge curtain by the sound of it. A penetrated curtain.

Is it music? Oh, is it ever!

Hear the wonder? The wonder of worship by people now close to their God? They're streaming in. Listen to the joy! Children, laborers, and homemakers standing in the holy of holies for the first time ever!

He has done it, that silent man hanging there on the cross. You wouldn't know it from the way he looks. Wouldn't know it from the soldiers' glee.

But he has done it. He has played it.

Can you hear it?

Matthew 27:50–56; Ephesians 2:11–18; Colossians 2:13–15; Hebrews 10:19–22

FOR REFLECTION: Do I hear the symphony playing in my life?

IN REMEMBRANCE

My head in a cloud of confusion and remorse, I found myself wandering up the trail to the Skull. Had it really happened to him?

I walked the stony terrain overlooking the city that had mocked him as with a single voice and expunged him from her streets in an evil hysteria.

I looked down at my feet and saw that I was standing on a discolored patch of rock. His blood was dry now. Flies buzzed around it.

My mind reluctantly reproduced the image of ugliness: his limp body falling into the uncaring arms of soldiers in the creeping shadows of dusk. Though his bones had been spared, his body was completely broken. So much hope carried off as a corpse.

And his blood had flowed down, from head and hands and feet and side, dripping on the place I now stood. It had even forced its way out through the very pores of his skin. Blood was everywhere.

How did it come to this?

My jaw hurt with yet another urge to weep.

Could it have been but thirty-six hours ago that we sat together in the upper room, celebrating the Passover together? Was he still with us such a short time ago?

Oh, that I could go back. If I had only realized then how little time was left.

I remember thinking it odd how, almost midsentence, he stopped everything. A solemn mood fell over him, and he slowly looked around the table from face to face.

Almost reverently he reached for a small loaf of bread. He held it out and prayed. How he prayed! Strange that he should be so very thankful for something as common as bread. Thankful that it gives life. Thankful that it satisfies.

I saw no special significance in his breaking the bread other than the way he did it. And when he gave it to us, I only thought it unusual that he said, "Take it; this is my body." Likewise with the cup. "This is my blood of the covenant, which is poured out for many."

Puzzling.

I scooped up a handful of rocks and threw them in disgust. I spit out my frustration. "You could have avoided Jerusalem! You could have escaped! Look where you are now. Your flesh is rotting in a tomb. Your blood a meal for flies. What a waste!"

There was nowhere I wanted to go, no one I wanted to talk to. The place felt heavy with the lingering depression of execution. Yet I wasn't ready to leave. I decided to sit down right there and rest my weakening legs, and before long I was sleeping fitfully.

At dusk I awoke to the mental image of a woman's face. I had been dreaming of her. She was familiar to me, but I couldn't place her at first. As my head cleared, it came to me: She was the one we had scolded. Not without cause, for she seemed to have lost her mind, pouring such costly perfume all out, and all at once, on the Master's head. And so much of it! We couldn't believe the misuse.

But Jesus—always coming when we were going, forever surprising us with his responses—Jesus appreciated her. "She has done a beautiful thing to me."

I stared down at the blood-dyed cracks. I recalled him breaking the bread. I pictured him sagging lifelessly on the cross. And the fog of my mind lifted.

She broke open the vial and poured out the expensive ointment.

And so did he.

My knees buckled, and I slumped to the granite of Golgotha.

Alabaster broken and precious perfume applied. Extravagant!

My Lord broken, his priceless life poured out. Incomprehensible!

My tears, finally uncontained, dropped unevenly on the red stains below.

O blessed waste!

Mark 14:3–9, 22–25

FOR REFLECTION: What extravagance have I poured out on Jesus lately? Do I appreciate the extravagance he has poured out on me?

PART FOUR

In the Dissipating Mists of a New Dawn

Finally, the precipitating tension of the story breaks. The turmoil settles. And the tale of your friendship with Christ enters into chapters with titles such as Peace, Clarity, and Resolve.

You endured the night watch together. Now share the joy of his victory.

The long night of suffering is over. The dawn is breaking. A call has gone forth into the night. The first rays have been summoned...by resurrection.

The rising sun mercilessly chases the fog away, replacing your limited view with clarity. Confusion flees before the rapid footsteps of insight and purposefulness. Your friendship with Christ takes flight, your songs of joy are somehow clearer and sweeter in the crisp air of sunup. The times of walking the midday paths seem distant. But they were not that long ago. You and he have been together through the long, hard night. You have emerged together on the other side, your relationship stronger than ever.

Jesus invites you to join him in the bright prospect of a new day. No matter how long you've been in the darkness, no matter how overdue the first light seems, he says "come" to a fresh new level of friendship.

What does the new dawn mean? It means Hope. Responsibility. And Intimacy.

Hope, because the story of your relationship did not end on a wooden cross. And because you still have so much yet to discover, discovery which holds for you wonder and glory and reunion.

Responsibility, because Jesus is alive, and that leaves no room for life as usual. Jesus has risen, and an unresurrected humanity needs to know. So now we're responsible to persevere, to live radically. If the hope of the resurrection makes suicide appealing, the demands of the resurrection render it wasteful.

And Intimacy. Intimacy of friendship never before known, both in quality and extent. So intimate that he can now do more than walk paths with you; the glorified Jesus can live within you. Now he moves you into the level of the eternal to see the previously hidden, to know the previously veiled, to live with him forever.

And, gloriously, here the analogy breaks down. A friendship is like a story, except that stories must end. Friendship with Christ does not. The final chapters reveal that they're not final at all. They only bring to a close the first book in an infinitely long set of volumes that fills row after row of shelves as far as the eye can see.

Is it any wonder that Jesus beckons you to meet him past the cross? Are you at all surprised that he wants you to experience what comes after his suffering and humiliation? The majesties and adventures he reserves for you to see?

Knowing him as you do, it makes perfect sense, doesn't it?

So picture the scene. He has anticipation written all over his face. He takes your hand, never to let go again. He moves out, his stride firm and expectant, bringing you into the world he has wanted to show you since before you were born.

Lace up for adventure, and don't let go!

CHAPTER SEVENTEEN

IMAGINE HIM RISING AGAIN FOR YOU

How did it happen in the tomb, that unlikely holy of holies?

Was it a gradual awakening, starting with a toe twitching or an eye winking?

Or did he just sit up all at once?

Either way, Jesus Christ, with the wax seal on his death certificate well past dried, came back to life. His puncture wounds began their healing process. Stiffened arteries began to loosen again with the movement of warm red blood. A chorus in miniature, his veins awakened, set in motion by the Conductor's downbeat.

Thoughts returned. (What was his first thought? I wonder.)

Hunger was there as proof of life.

In short, living matter replaced dead. Decomposition gave way to creation. And while hell shuddered, all heaven and nature sang.

Why? Because Jesus Christ's resurrection from the jaws of death makes all the difference.

It separates Jesus from a host of other fine teachers and people movers. It marks him as different from any other world leader, religious or otherwise.

If Jesus is not risen, we are duped participants in the greatest deception of human history, bar none. But if he is, then we've won the biggest gamble ever taken with the biggest prize ever offered.

No wonder all hell assaults the idea. No wonder even our own minds scream out at times against the improbability of it all. No wonder Mohammed and Krishna and Confucius and Buddha and Baal (by whatever modern name) all line up to mock the very concept of the resurrection.

It is the fulcrum of eternity. It is the crux of the battle between falsehood and truth. It is the Red Sea of your spiritual pilgrimage.

And it happened in that most holy place.

REUNION!

With the force of seven demons, the feelings of despair, confusion, and discouragement returned with the stealth of nighttime intruders. Robbers of hope and stability struck with surprise. They burglarized her of her peace.

And it happened just as her protector was nowhere to be found. Jesus had become not only her deliverer but her ongoing source of strength. She had grown accustomed to looking to him for help during these times of fright.

How she needed him now. But where was he?

Gone. Unavailable. Taken unexpectedly.

He had left such a void in her life. No one could ever fill his place. There was no other like him.

Does anyone miss him the way I do? Has anyone been changed by his love as much as I have? Or am I completely alone? Doesn't anyone else share my loneliness?

Perhaps that's why she lingered alone where he had last been seen. Walked the paths which possibly bore his final footprints. Ran her fingers along the place he had last touched. Hoped that he might somehow appear.

Could he have forgotten about her? Was she not so important to him after all? *So many loved him, and he loved so many. How foolish of me to expect any special treatment.*

All things considered, it happened at the perfect time.

Reunion.

He came to her as one unrecognized. (*I thought I knew everything about him.)* She had prescribed his appearing by expecting the routine. But he still held the knack for surprise.

His return was so nonchalant it gave her the feeling that she had only imagined him as remote. Had he ever been that far away?

So alive and real! It was as if the veil of separation had only served to make his presence more fulfilling. The joy of rediscovery vindicated the pain of separation.

The assurance of his voice confirmed for her the reality of his nearness. (Do they who long for him most hear his voice first?) He was still the same. Still the comforter.

The band of intruders now knew they'd been discovered and overpowered. She was not defenseless as they had supposed. The house was not empty after all.

They slithered out the doors, let go of the areas they had begun to seize once again.

She was at home. He was with her again, never to leave.

She was safe.

Matthew 12:43–45; Mark 16:9–11; John 20:1–18

FOR REFLECTION: Am I enjoying the reality of his comfort? Has loneliness produced in me the fruit of joy?

BURNING HEARTS

Then their eyes were opened and they recognized him,
and he disappeared from their sight.
They asked each other, "Were not our hearts burning within us
while he talked with us on the road
and opened the Scriptures to us?"
LUKE 24:31–32

Two men walked to the front of the house, one preparing to leave for his own home and a well-deserved night's sleep. It was late, the end of a full and unforgettable evening.

"I'm glad you were there tonight, my friend. Otherwise I'd be tempted to think it didn't really happen. You and I must be the most privileged fellows on earth to have a personal tutorial from the Lord."

"I agree completely. Never before have I seen the Scriptures the way I do now. It makes so much sense when you see it through his eyes. And to see how often Moses and the prophets predicted Christ's ministry, even down to details like nails in his hands and feet!"

"And the words he would say on the cross."

The brothers in faith found it difficult to get off the subject. One recalled his amazement when he realized that Jesus fulfilled the judgment God made on Satan in the Garden of Eden—that Satan would succeed in injuring Christ but that Christ would destroy Satan completely. The other had to bring up the amazing parallels of Jesus as the Passover Lamb—how God had clearly described the kind of Savior the people should expect: a man like an unblemished lamb, with deliverance based on shed blood, with not a bone of his body broken.

"I don't know if I can describe it, but my heart burned with excitement over who my Savior truly is..."

"Yes, I know. Never again will I doubt that he is truly the Christ or that he has risen from the dead."

"Remember *Jehovah-Jireh,* the Lord will provide? Isaac willingly entrusted his life to his father Abraham, but Christ was both willing and adequate as a sacrifice. It hit me like a hammer blow that I could personally know the sacrificial provision we have awaited for centuries!"

"The words of Isaiah nearly made me choke. I was so amazed at how deeply they described Jesus' ultimate work. I can nearly quote them: 'Surely he took up our infirmities and carried our sorrows, yet we considered him stricken by God, smitten by him, and afflicted. But he was pierced for our transgressions, he was crushed for our iniquities; the punishment that brought us peace was upon him, and by his wounds we are healed.'"

What could cause two grown men to stand under the stars and discuss ancient Scripture passages? Was it not the fact that they had been in the presence of the one whom those Scriptures foretold, the one about whom all the prophets wrote, the one at whom angels so marveled that they longed to look into and understand his work?

These men had been on holy ground. Their hearts burned with wholesome passion for the Son of God.

Finally they had to part company. The one who was leaving closed the car door. Turning the ignition key, the engine rumbled to life.

"Let's study the Word again next week. Same time?"

"Wouldn't miss it."

Luke 24:13–32; Genesis 3:15; 22:8, 14; Exodus 12:5–7, 13, 46; Psalm 22:1, 16, 18; Isaiah 53:4–5

FOR REFLECTION: Do I believe that the Savior who walked and taught on the Emmaus road is the same one who desires to converse with me now?

THE KING RETURNS

"He has been given the Name!"

Never before had a single piece of news spread so fast and so widely. In a moment's time the message reverberated throughout the heavens, the earth, and under the earth.

All the angels knew it. As soon as they heard, they began rushing toward the throne room.

Legions upon legions of demons heard it, too. They had gathered from unofficial sources that this might happen, but how could he have actually done it, and so suddenly? Apollyon had told them that the Name was not truly accessible to anyone, that it was just a legend from ancient times, a trick of God to spread fear throughout the kingdom of darkness.

But now it appeared their worst fear had come true. The chief deceiver in their own camp had lived up to his name. They screeched in terror, for they knew their plight: powerlessness. Their fate was sealed unalterably.

Meanwhile, the throne room of God couldn't have carried a more contrasting mood. Everyone moved about in celebrative anticipation of the Son's return.

Choirs rehearsed one after the other. "Worthy is the Lamb who was slain..." and then, "Who is able to open the Book? Only the Lion of Judah..."

The twenty-four elders were beside themselves in praise. They could not contain their proclamations. Such preaching you have never heard: The Son had tasted death for everyone, they said. Now he was to be crowned with glory and honor as he had been before. He had been given the Name above every name, they said.

The sea of glass seemed more brilliant than ever. You could see reflected in it the words inscribed on the foundation of God's throne: "The Lord knows those who are his. Everyone who confesses the name of the Lord must turn away from wickedness."

Suddenly a hush fell over everyone. Instinctively all eyes turned toward the Great Colonnade. Necks stretched to see. Through the mist you could see a clearing being made for the One all had waited for.

The King had returned! It was true: The Son of God had indeed risen from the dead!

He wore a simple white robe, glowing in righteousness. He was the same as always, but somehow different, too. God the Son was also a man.

You could see in his countenance compassion born of suffering. You could see scars on his body. He made no attempt to hide them.

He carried nothing, except that in his right hand he held keys. What locks would they open? The answer came as Jesus walked toward the throne, for behind him was a procession of the most jubilant men, women, and children you could ever hope to see. They jumped and sang. They waved and hooted. They were freed captives. So that was it. Jesus had won the keys to death and Hades!

As the King led his triumphal parade, a spontaneous reaction arose that required no cue or signal. Unprompted, everyone bowed to their knees.

As the Son approached the throne, the Father looked at him with pride. And well he should, for what he saw in his Son was Lordship from head to foot.

The Father put a glorious robe upon the Son's shoulders. And upon his head the Crown of Honor.

The Father spoke, "I give you the name that is given to no other. I give you the name that sets the captives free. I give you the name to which all must submit. I give you the name, Jesus Christ the Lord."

It's a good thing that clocks do not tick in heaven, for the cheering went on forever.

At last the Father nodded to the Son with a smile meant to congratulate.

And in response Jesus Christ sat down at the right hand of God. Yes, the Son of God sat down.

The place came apart at the seams with praise!

And the celebration only increased as Jesus did the unexpected. He motioned to the freed captives he had brought with him. He gathered them all and set them on his throne with him.

By and by, those he had set free broke out in song:

> If we died with him, we will also live with him;
>   if we endure, we will also reign with him.
> If we disown him, he will also disown us;
>   if we are faithless, he will remain faithful,
>   for he cannot disown himself.

It was clear they sang to a distant throng, to others still on the way.

Thinking of that future day, the Son grinned at the Father. He knew that there would be a time, though not in time, when every knee would bow and every tongue confess that Jesus Christ is Lord, to the glory of God the Father.

Philippians 2:9–11; 2 Timothy 2:11–13, 19

FOR REFLECTION: When I bow, will it be in the shame of defeat or in the joy of sharing his victory?

CHAPTER EIGHTEEN

IMAGINE HIM SENDING YOU

Our lives are a continuation of the mission Jesus began. In fact, our commission to tell his story is evidence of his success.

Think about it this way...

If he hadn't come in the first place, we wouldn't have any reason to go in his name.

Or if he had failed, he wouldn't need us, for there'd be no work to carry on.

Or consider: If the good news weren't really that good, Christ's sending us would be worthless.

If he had no confidence in us, he would not have entrusted us with the message.

And if no one else wanted to hear the news, there'd be no point in telling it.

But he did come.

He did succeed.

The message is wonderful, he trusts us to tell it, and many long to hear it.

It's a success story in the making.

THE PLAN UNBEATABLE

Then he said to his disciples, "The harvest is plentiful
but the workers are few.
Ask the Lord of the harvest, therefore,
to send out workers into his harvest field."

MATTHEW 9:37–38

In your Bible these verses are followed by a space which alerts you to the beginning of a new chapter. Maybe that interval represents twelve minutes. Or perhaps twelve days.

Let's have it represent a conversation between twelve men and their Leader. As you'll notice, they weren't exactly seeing eye to eye....

"We've been thinking about your need for more workers. We really empathize with your frustration. In fact, we've put in some extra time planning how this venture can come together."

"Good! I always have an open ear for creative thinking."

"We feel the whole operation needs to rest on the foundation of the right strategy. Choosing the appropriate target audience—that's the key. Having thought it over, we can give ourselves the best chance of starting a movement if we aim at those basically well established in life. When we win them over, they'll give the right impression as to the kind of group we are."

"I see."

"And then there's the matter of finances. This endeavor will obviously require funding. We figure we need to begin immediately developing a strong support base right here in Galilee. That way the laborers you recruit won't have to worry about their day-to-day expenses. We can also give them some training in generating supplemental income from among those they minister to. What do you think so far?"

"To be honest, your ideas aren't quite in line with my own. I tend to think that these laborers will minister to the hurting rather than the well placed. And on the financial issue, I have in mind a rather low-budget operation. But maybe some of your other ideas will hit closer to the mark."

"We agreed that it would be a mistake to send out these recruits undersupplied. With the right kind of planning, they should be able to carry with them all the provisions they'll need to complete the entire assignment. Our consensus was that it gives the wrong impression to depend on others along the way for basic necessities. We don't want our people to get into the bind of being beyond their resources.

"Which leads to another area of planning we've considered. The training program ought to be very thorough, covering any and every eventuality they might run into. They ought to know in advance what to say in every situation. Leave nothing to improvisation—that's the key. We feel they ought to be protected from any embarrassment."

"Interesting ideas, fellows. Thorough and, may I say, natural. But again, I have a different style of ministry in mind. I want my laborers to depend on me completely. That means carrying no money, not even a wallet. And as for planning speeches, the Spirit will supply the words when and wherever they're needed."

"Lord, this is most surprising. At least you must agree with our thinking that our top priority in this venture must be to win acceptance of your message at any cost. We don't want these workers returning with reports of too many failures. If they can keep from offending anyone and make the good news palatable to as many as possible, then we'll have run a successful campaign. Don't you agree, Master?"

"I think perhaps you should have planned a little less and prayed a little more."

"Why do you say that?"

"Praying might have revealed a better plan."

"Better plan? Lord, with all due respect, it seems that anyone going out under your plan is basically a sheep walking into a pack of wolves!"

"I doubt I could have said it better myself."

"Those poor recruits will be fleeing from one city to the next."

"Yes, I know."

"Where in the world do you plan to find such people? Few of us would offer even our *distant* relatives for that kind of assignment."

"I know a few who will go. They have come to care for the multitudes the way I do. They see the lost as scattered and shepherdless sheep. They will lack many provisions. They won't have any sophisticated plans. But they *will* have authority to heal the sick and cast out demons."

"How many of these guys do you know?"

"Just twelve."

One or two of them stirred. "And where would they be getting this authority?"

"From me."

Several seemed to have throat congestion which needed clearing. "Would we happen to have made their acquaintance yet?"

"Indeed."

Insight was well into dawning. The disciples slowly eyed one another. Uncharacteristic silence lingered. Until…

"Not even a wallet?"

Matthew 9:35–10:23

FOR REFLECTION: Am I planning my way instead of praying for his?

A TRUST SO SACRED

Eleven men—searching, along with a host of others, for moorings in the windy channel between Passover and Pentecost—had gone ahead to the mountain location Jesus had told them about.

There they waited, according to his direction. Their aimlessness evidenced itself in curt replies and sleepiness. They needed to see their Master again.

Meanwhile Jesus was beginning his journey up the mountain. When he came to the first turn of the winding trail, Satan met him. "I've seen your followers on the mountain. They're ready for you. They're a good group, I can see that...especially once they get themselves organized. I'm afraid I won't be able to stop them."

"That's right," Jesus replied. "You won't be able to overcome them."

The Lord walked past his adversary undaunted.

Soon he came to a river where he took a moment to stop for a refreshing drink. In anticipation, Satan had placed himself at a nearby bush. "I wish I could have stopped you from going to the cross. I didn't see it for what it was. You really tricked me on that one. Now your followers have the message that changes lives. I should have defeated you while there was just you. Now I'm up against hundreds. Impossible!"

Jesus gasped for air after a satisfying drink and wiped his mouth with the back of his wrist. "Don't patronize me, Satan. They've got the truth, and it will forever oppose your lies. And the life they have to share will depopulate your kingdom of deception."

The path widened into a small meadow. Jesus took in the sunshine. Satan, having positioned himself on an old log, continued his empty flattery: "Sending them out in your place makes a lot of sense. After all, you're only one person; you can't travel around that much. But they'll be able to go everywhere. Yes, your idea is truly a stroke of genius."

"You don't know the half. I'm not doing this because I'm unable. I'm doing it because I value their contribution. I believe in them."

"Oh yes, by all means," Satan feigned agreement. "I'm sure they won't let you down. This is a sad day for me."

"You don't fool me," Jesus said as he gladly passed out of hearing range.

He knew by now that he was nearing the designated place. He thought of it with pleasure.

But Satan had not completed his charade. "It probably sounds funny, but I'm beginning to see it your way. You didn't just come to do everything yourself. You came to earth to do your part. Now that you've done that, you're sending them out to do their part. They'll be able to reflect back on the things you said to them. And of course they'll be able to support one another...so they won't be alone or anything."

"You've enjoyed centuries of domination over nations. I'm not naive enough to think that you're going to relinquish them without a fight. So I'm sending my disciples out, yes. But not alone. I'm going with them, and I'm giving them my name."

"Yes, I'm trying to get used to that," replied Satan. "It will be difficult to have so many people following your name. I'm bolstering myself against the prospect of even whole nations declaring allegiance to you."

"Easy allegiance means little to me. I'm not content with mere lip service or casual converts. These that I am sending will win and train *true* followers. They'll know the difference."

"I'm sure they will. And for that very reason I think you're wise to place your hope squarely on them. Having a backup plan would communicate a lack of confidence in their ability. Very intelligent. You've really outsmarted me this time."

Jesus came up the trail to a rise. In front of him was the gathering of disciples. He knew that some of them were merely curious, not really committed. Some even doubted whether he had truly risen from the dead.

Satan approached him. Looking at the rather motley gathering, he smiled wryly. "There they are, the future of your kingdom."

Jesus waved him off, tired of the caper. He grinned confidently and walked toward his disciples. As often as he had had to tell his followers not to spread the word about him, there was a certain pleasure in this event. He was filled with expectation and hope.

After he had invited them to sit down, Jesus explained to the disciples about his authority. He told them he no longer had any legitimate opponent. There was no information floating around that anyone could use to bring him down, no speck of power he did not possess. No eventuality would ever surprise him. No region of heaven or earth stood outside his rightful authority. No flaw could ever be shown in his character or his finished work. No oversight would ever render him mistaken.

"That's why I'm so confident in sending you out to represent me. If you stay faithful, you cannot possibly fail."

Then at last he made it official—what he had been leading up to all along. He told them to go—to go from comfort to risk, from caring little to caring intensely for those who needed him. He told them never to stop going.

And he told them they would never be alone.

He thought back to the time he was sent from heaven. And it filled him with confidence, for he knew they would have his spirit, the spirit of adventure.

Matthew 28:16–20

FOR REFLECTION: Do I share my Savior's confidence that the job will be done?

CHAPTER NINETEEN

IMAGINE HIM INTERCEDING FOR YOU

Some people seem to think that Jesus has gone into semiretirement, that sitting down at the Father's right hand means Jesus kicked off his shoes, ordered his favorite beverage, and now enjoys the angels pampering him until his services are again required.

Let's agree that Jesus certainly *deserves* such treatment. But let's hastily thank him for refusing it.

Explanation forthcoming.

The author of Hebrews rejoices in the extent of our salvation by saying: "Therefore he is able to save completely those who come to God through him..." (Hebrews 7:25). The Greek word translated "completely" has the idea of "entirely" or even "finally." In other words, the salvation Christ has provided doesn't fall short in any way, either in quality or thoroughness.

But it's the end of the verse that I'm driving toward: "...because he always lives to intercede for them." By what reason, or on what basis, is our salvation complete in Christ? Answer: He still lives and intercedes for the ones he has saved. (Ready for this?) He *is saving* us through his present ministry of intercession.

Meaning what?

To intercede is to make petition. That is, to ask or request. I take it that Jesus is constantly praying for you and me, praying for everything we need to stand in grace and to walk in faith.

Call it theological speculation if you like (check me out), but I read the Bible to say that every millisecond you continue to enjoy salvation depends entirely and solely on the present ministry of Jesus Christ in heaven (and against hell). I can't fathom all it involves, and I certainly can't explain it fully. But I think we have a Savior who is, at this moment, doggedly refusing to lose even one precious person who has come to him by faith for salvation. And I figure that's the only reason you and I possess even an ounce of commitment right now.

Semiretirement? What a joke!

THE DREAMER

Circa 1160 B.C. Somewhere in Palestine

The younger priest had been apprenticed to the older because the latter had a recognized gift of tolerance.

Caleb saw his assignment in the tabernacle differently than his contemporaries. They viewed it as the fulfillment of a dream, a post to fill till death. But the tabernacle was Caleb's classroom and Ezri his teacher. Others interpreted Caleb's incessant wondering as impertinence. Fortunately Ezri saw it more as potential. But still, the teacher knew that restraint was the main lesson Caleb needed to learn.

"Polish those candlesticks till you could see a flock of goats in them. Yom Kippur is only a month away, and I won't have anything looking second-rate."

"Don't worry, Ezri. They'll gleam so brightly that even your fading eyes could see the reflection of Mount Horeb in them! Speaking of getting along in years, how is the high priest's health these days? Will he be strong enough for the Day of Atonement?"

"He's improving, I hear. May God raise him to full health so he may perform his sacred duty."

"Ezri, my faithful mentor, I've just been thinking. Wouldn't it be something if we had a high priest who never became ill? Or better yet, one who would never die but would stand before God continually as our mediator?"

"Ha! Now there's one I haven't heard before! You've outdone yourself this time, Caleb. But I wouldn't spread that particular suggestion around the community if I were you. The high priest might somehow misunderstand your good intentions."

"Rebellion is the last thing on my mind, Ezri. I'm simply taking an honest look at the many limitations we face in this ministry."

"Mmmm."

"We priests are a case in point. Who are *we* to offer sacrifices for the people? We have to present sacrifices for ourselves! Even the high priest, when he enters the Holy of Holies in a month's time, will first have to seek God's cleansing for himself."

"That's the system, Caleb. Criticize the system, and you criticize God."

"But is this system God's first choice? The endless cycle of it all? When a priest dies, he has to be replaced. Wouldn't it be a relief, even to Jehovah, to have just one high priest for all time? And think of the sacrifices. Over and over, day after day, we have to offer God these things. I'm not criticizing, Ezri. Just thinking out loud: If the sacrifices were really doing something, couldn't we stop offering them?"

"Sure, if people would just quit sinning."

"Yes, that's a problem. But, Ezri, if the blood of bulls and goats really takes away sin, why do I go away from the altar still feeling guilty? It seems the sacrifices just *remind* me of what a transgressor I am."

"Uh-oh, you may be beyond help. We'll have to—"

"Oh, be quiet, Ezri. You know good and well what I mean, and you've felt the same way, haven't you?"

"Well, yes."

"What we need, Ezri, is a better covenant."

"Now that's enough, you young dreamer! You're speaking heresy, and that I cannot tolerate. Plus, the things you're saying are impossible. You want a high priest who doesn't get sick or die, who doesn't have any sin himself. You want sacrifices that don't have to be offered continually, and you want them to actually remove guilty feelings. Well, young one, where are you going to find a tabernacle like that? Heaven?"

"Hmmm, you may be onto something there, Ezri! Heaven *is* the logical place. *Anything* can happen *there.*"

"But then it doesn't do *us* any good down here, does it, Caleb?"

"You never know. Prayer bridges the gap. Why not a heavenly tabernacle?"

"You've lost your mind—and at such a young age, too!"

Caleb's mind was reeling. "That would mean it would be a tabernacle made by God, not man. Hey, Ezri, we wouldn't have to polish candlesticks!"

"Thanks for reminding me. Get to work!"

"And the high priest wouldn't have human limitations. He wouldn't die. He wouldn't have to atone for his own sins. And just one of his sacrifices would suffice for everyone for all time! It would work, Ezri. It would truly take away the guilt of sin."

The old man put down the scroll he had been trying to read and looked straight at Caleb (who returned the favor). "When did you go mad? Was it a gradual thing, or were you born this way?"

"Ezri, one thing I've always liked about you is your sense of humor. Trouble is, I'm trying but I don't *sense* any *humor* around here right now. Get it?"

"Okay, if you think your idea is so perfect, I've got a question for *you* for a change: Who will make this sacrifice and live to tell about it? You seem to have forgotten, Sir Genius, that a sacrifice is a one-time affair."

"Yes, you have a point there, Ezri. That is a *major* problem."

"Thank you."

"But, Ezri, humor me on this one: If somehow a high priest could be sinless and eternal and able to permanently forgive us, what would you say?"

The aging priest looked at his scroll. "Officially I would say it's impossible—end of discussion. But unofficially, just between you, me, and the curtain…it would be too wonderful to imagine!"

Hebrews 7:23–8:13; 9:23–10:25
FOR REFLECTION: How do I feel when I realize that Christ has done the impossible?

RAP OF THE GAVEL

It happened yesterday and the day before that.

It has happened already today: Your name was mentioned in heaven.

Unfortunately your name wasn't mentioned in a friendly context. No, an accuser approached God the Father and brought up a plethora of charges against you. Charges of failure and unforgiveness and gossip and envy and pride and rebelliousness. On and on went his list of reasons why you should no longer enjoy God's good graces.

This accuser claimed that the basis for the charges was the law of sin and death. When asked to define this law, your accuser said that because you were once a sinner, you'll always be a sinner, that sin will eventually get you in the end, and that you're basically a bad person.

The Father wasn't impressed. He turned to your Advocate for confirmation of what he already knew. In response, Jesus replied, "Some of these charges are true; others are deceptions. Either way, Your Honor, all charges against your child are covered by my shed blood."

The gavel came down with a thump. "All charges dismissed!"

Your accuser then took a different tack. He brought up all sorts of condemnation. He assaulted your character viciously. He said that although you always say you want to do good, you are always and without exception favoring evil. He accused you of pretending to delight in God's ways but in truth remaining a prisoner of sin. He scoffed, wondering how God could continue to put up with a wretch like you.

Once again he appealed to the law of sin and death, quoting it (apparently) as saying that your body is programmed for death, that ever since the fall of humankind you have signed away your life to the condemnation of your sin.

God the Father hated to hear such words used about you. But he took confident delight in the playing out of this courtroom drama. As Judge, he knew he had absolute control over the outcome. And he also knew all the evidence beforehand. He looked at your Intercessor with the assurance of one who couldn't possibly be surprised.

Jesus replied, "Of course, Your Honor, everyone knows that the body of death is bent toward evil. There's no hope in trying to improve it. But the accuser has chosen once again to ignore the fact that I've rescued my child from the body of death. All these condemnations are covered by my resurrection."

The gavel came down. "All condemnations dismissed!"

But your accuser didn't know when to quit. He revealed his desperation by making a host of threats against you. He whined that because the Judge had not paid any attention, he, your accuser, would bring trouble and hardship on you and your loved ones. He threatened to persecute you and make you suffer loss. He smirked, saying he would enlist the help of other demons and even higher powers to destroy you. All this, he claimed, would drive a wedge between God and you, his child. These troubles would cut you off from God's love.

At this statement the Father had to muffle his laughter. Holding his tongue, he looked to the Victor knowingly. In response Jesus said, "Actually, Your Honor, these threats are an absolute impossibility. There's no way on heaven or earth, no way in time or eternity, that I would let this peon come between you and your child. My love and my undisputed power over this accuser's master will span any distance to protect my friend. Neither death nor life, neither angels nor demons, neither the present nor the future, nor any powers, neither height nor depth, nor anything else in all creation can separate us from this beloved child of ours. Ever!"

The gavel came down with a finality that signaled the end of your accuser's access to the Judge. "All threats dismissed!"

Discouraged, the accuser thought unkindly of his leader, Apollyon, who continually sent him on these missions. *Doesn't the fool know what all of us foot soldiers know by now, that we have no basis for accusing or condemning these children of God? Hasn't he gotten it by now, that you cannot shake the Victor's confidence with threats? The law of sin and death? Ha! What a joke. It doesn't carry any weight in heaven. Guess I'll go back to my old faithful strategy...*

Moments later you awake to face a new day. You think about the challenges you face. You remember some of your difficulties and past failures.

Once a sinner, always a sinner. Sin will always get me in the end. I'm just no good.

You marvel at the recurring nature of your negative thoughts.

I'm programmed to sin. I'm fallen. I can't possibly overcome my bodily desires to sin. Though I asked forgiveness yesterday, I'll only fail again today.

What will you do? Will you fix your mind on what's happening in heaven or on earth?

Romans 7:21–25; 8:1, 31–39; 1 John 2:1–2
FOR REFLECTION: Do I live in the confidence that my Advocate in heaven defends me daily?

CHAPTER TWENTY

IMAGINE HIM LIVING INSIDE YOU

If you could experience one moment in Christ's ministry, which would you choose?

Would you want to hear him say, *"Talitha koum!"* and see the joy on two parents' faces as they received back their daughter (Mark 5:41)? Would you witness Jesus overturning the moneychangers' tables in the temple and see in their expressions a recognition of true authority?

Wouldn't it be wonderful to live in Christ's time and to actually be where he lived and worked?

Yes, it would.

And yes, it *is.*

I say "is" because of a well-kept secret of the Bible: Jesus has placed his very own Spirit—the Spirit who raised the twelve-year-old and drove out the charlatans—in all who believe in Him.

The Lord didn't intend this to be a secret:

- "I will not leave you as orphans; I will come to you" (John 14:18).
- "Remain in me, and I will remain in you" (John 15:4).
- "In a little while you will see me no more, and then after a little while you will see me" (John 16:16).
- The "Spirit of Jesus" directly intervened and prevented Paul from

going to Bithynia (Acts 16:7), the same Spirit that encouraged Paul in prison (Philippians 1:19).

- The Spirit of Jesus works in us as adopted children, causing us to long for our heavenly Father (Galatians 4:6) and assuring us we belong to him (Roman 8:9).

So if you long to live as Christ's contemporary, you're living at a perfect time. He'll be in action *today.* And if you desire to be where he's at work, you couldn't be in a better place. He lives *right inside you.*

The secret is out. And when you think about it for a while, Jesus feels centuries closer. And you start wondering what he'll think and what he might do as he spends today with you.

Who knows, maybe you'll meet some overjoyed parents or a woman who touched his garment!

THE PROMISE MOST IGNORED (WITH THE BEST INTENTIONS)

To my dear friend Theophilus, a brief letter to inform you of the disappointing events of these days.

You can imagine the excitement that filled our number following the resurrection of our Lord. I do not think morale could have been any higher once we realized that Jesus himself had actually come back to life. My own heart was filled with unbounded optimism; I thought we were all ready to carry on during the interim Jesus would be away from us.

In my opinion we should capitalize on the momentum we currently enjoy among the group. We have so many things going in our favor. Specifically, some of us have planned a schedule of cities to visit first, and we feel we have arrived at the best strategy possible. We have no shortage of personnel at the moment, for, as I said, enthusiasm for telling others is wonderful. Our biggest asset of course is our message, the good news that changes lives.

This leads me to tell you of my concern. Jesus has told us to wait in Jerusalem. I am completely baffled by this idea. And just when we have widespread interest all around the country! Even in the smallest villages you can hear talk of the resurrection. Waiting will mean a loss of interest on the part of our volunteers, and before we know it, we will find ourselves having to recruit new people to fill the ranks. I feel an urgency that the Lord doesn't seem to share.

An additional burden on my heart is that other communities are working hard for converts to their causes. They are probably getting so far ahead we'll never catch up.

None of the great endeavors we hear about are known for waiting. Zeal has always been the hallmark of success. Remember the group that really stole the thunder of the religious world not long ago? They had good strategy. They recruited the most pleasing personnel. They were simply a sharp enterprise.

I guess I had hoped we would make a similar impact. But here we are waiting around, and in Jerusalem of all places! This city has a hard heart. They had the very Lord himself here, and they crucified him. What does Jesus think we can do that he couldn't? Everyone interested in Christ has surely heard about him and has already accepted him. The rest are happy without him and aren't likely to be persuaded otherwise.

It seems to me, brother, that we ought to be in Phoenicia by now, not cooped up here in this overexposed city that will never respond. Didn't Jesus tell us to go to those ripe harvest fields? Either that or we should be on our way to places where the gospel hasn't even reached yet to give those people a chance.

I'm sure my disappointment is obvious. Don't get me wrong. I'm not angry with the Lord, just perplexed. I thought he was a better strategist than what I'm seeing in him these days. And I anticipated more courage from him, too.

Once he departs, I hope he returns in just a few days because at this rate, we'll have a hard time hanging on very much longer than that.

Sorry to close this letter on a low note, but I've always been able to confide in you. Please pray for us, brother.

PS My friend, a few additional words. Please disregard the above letter. I could not have been more wrong about waiting. Today was Pentecost. Suffice it to say that my plan would not only have meant our failure but the unraveling of the whole operation. I had no idea that our waiting meant

Jesus giving us his own power for ministry. It will make all the difference. I'll send you a full report with the details. My, am I glad I'm not in charge!

Luke 24:44–49; Acts 1:3–14; 2:1–41

FOR REFLECTION: What would my life and ministry be like if I insisted on having Jesus' presence and power within me before moving forward?

THE JESUS PROBLEM

"I will not leave you as orphans; I will come to you.
Before long, the world will not see me anymore, but you will see me.
Because I live, you also will live.
On that day you will realize that I am in my Father, and you are in me, and I am in you."

JOHN 14:18–20

The members of the Sanhedrin filed in at random, gradually filling the semicircular chamber. Sitting on the crescent of benches, they had debated many issues. The fate of many accused had hung in the balance.

Today would be no exception.

Annas, the high priest, and Caiaphas, his son-in-law, entered and received their complimentary nods of respect. They had been the masterminds of many convenient judgments, including the disposal of Jesus, the self-proclaimed messiah.

Their adequate adjustment in their reserved seats signaled the time for calling the accused. Two men, Peter and John, entered with a third who stood for the first time on two strong legs.

Annas looked them over. *Who are these men? Peasant fishermen, it appears to me. They're probably accusing each other of territorial violations. But why would they come all the way to Jerusalem? And why clutter up my precious schedule with their petty disputes?*

Others in the council appeared to recognize the two. A chorus of muttering rounded the benches.

"All right, quiet!" Annas did not relish being less informed than his underlings. "Who are these men, and why are they before us?"

"They're here for creating a disturbance among the people," cried out a clerk.

The high priest was unaffected. *They don't look like revolutionaries, but then again we've had other unlikely candidates for glory stand before us on the very same spot.* "What kind of disturbance was it?"

"They were preaching in the temple..."

Temple orators! As common as old coins.

"...and they healed the man who stands with them, a man lame from birth."

When will the people begin to see through these bogus healers?

The clerk went on. "It appears the crowds were quite convinced that the man was actually healed."

The circle of Israel's leaders seemed to pause, almost as if reluctant to proceed. They had dealt with this problem before, all too recently in fact.

Finally, someone put voice to the question on every single mind. "By what power or in what name have you healed this man?"

Annas listened as the more outspoken of the two began his reply. The manner of his answer stirred up troubling emotions. *Why does this sound familiar? What's the connection?*

Words, rising in volume as the speaker gained confidence, pierced his thoughts like knives: "...that by the name of Jesus Christ the Nazarene whom you crucified, whom God raised from the dead—by this name this man stands before you in good health."

Protests and hollers erupted in the hall. Some laughed in manufactured mockery.

But the high priest sat in silence. He simply could not believe what he had heard. *The same kind of miracle. Same trouble among the people. Teaching with the same confidence. The same willingness to defy authority and endure suffering.*

The two disciples and their newest convert walked out of the chamber.

The council began their private deliberations behind closed doors, allowing those outside to believe that viable solutions were multiplying within. But inside, the kingdom builders knew, to a man, that their worst fears had just been confirmed: the Jesus problem would not go away.

Acts 4:1–22

FOR REFLECTION: How can I make it more obvious that I too have been with Jesus?

UNFORSAKEN

Reuel and I went back a long way with Jesus. We first heard him speak in the temple when he revealed himself as the light of the world. Both of us knew instantly that he was the Messiah. Though we never had the courage to speak to the Lord face to face, we followed him as often as we could. We loved him dearly and felt true affection from him.

I've always enjoyed a good memory. When Jesus was crucified, it caught us off guard for a while, until I remembered something he said when we first believed in him: that when the Son of Man was lifted up, we would know he was who he said he was.

So we knew that the Lord had only fulfilled his word, which of course his rising again reinforced a hundredfold. My, how we rejoiced during those days, knowing that our Lord was now reunited with his Father in heaven, that he had given us the authority of his name, and that his own Spirit was in fact living within us! The intimacy I felt with the Lord after his Spirit came was even greater than when we would edge our way through the Jerusalem crowds to hear him up close!

I must confess that our faith was really challenged when the trouble started. First, it was Stephen. Such a dear young man to die that way. But he placed his hope in the Lord, and he inspired us all to do the same. And how we needed to, because there followed a terrible explosion of violence against the Way by the religious leaders.

Lord, stay close to us during these fearful days. Don't let your presence seem far off.

Before long we began hearing a lot about a zealous man named Saul. He was young enough to be our son. We heard he would be so bold as to force his way into the homes of our brothers and sisters and confront everyone in the house, making them confess whether or not they belonged to Jesus.

In retrospect, our routine probably gave us away. We weren't exactly surreptitious by leaving the house every Sunday morning to go to our worship gathering! Late one Sunday night we heard loud banging and shouting at our door. It was Saul and some others as we had feared. Such an obnoxious person. But we had already decided that if anyone attacked us for our allegiance to Christ, we would not deny our Lord just to preserve our lifestyle.

They took Reuel to prison that night. (Thank the Lord I was able to stay calm.) *Lord, take care of Reuel. Be with him right there in prison. Fill him with your peace and serenity. Protect him from harm. Let him know the reality of your presence.*

Then, as now, Jesus was very real to me. I remember looking out our window toward the shop where Reuel used to work. I was filled with a confidence that my Lord was in control: "I am with you. I'll never leave or forsake you. Don't give up hope. I know just what you're going through." Jesus was right there with me; I have no doubt about that.

Later, after being beaten and threatened, Reuel was released. He told us that, though difficult, his time in prison had been a wonderful experience for him! *(Had he lost his mind?)* He said that he saw Jesus in prison in so many ways. "At one point the guards were taking me to the worst cell in the prison where I would have been badly beaten by the hardened criminals assigned there. But Jesus intervened through a guard sympathetic to the Way. Instead, I went to the same cell as the 'ruler' of the prison, who took good care of me. He even got me a blanket and some decent food. Esther, the Lord himself was in that prison with me!"

As I listened, I was filled with joy. But I also knew the Spirit of the Lord was dealing with me, and it felt uncomfortable. I still burned in my hatred for Saul. He had taken my husband. He had frightened me and our younger children. And for what? For the preservation of a lifeless orthodoxy. He wrongly saw us as weak-minded impostors, followers of a false messiah.

You can imagine how suspicious I was when I heard that Saul had become a believer in Christ! *Just like him. Worm his way into the inner workings of our assemblies and destroy us from within. Beware of that deceiver!*

I'll have to admit that Saul's conversion story did sound like something only the Lord could do. His voice coming from heaven like that must have really shocked the young tyrant: "Saul, Saul, why are you persecuting me?" My, I would have liked to have seen his face!

I suppose Saul couldn't imagine who the voice was talking about, but it makes perfect sense to me. I had even rehearsed my speech: "You were persecuting Jesus when you threw Reuel into prison and when you threatened me. You were persecuting Jesus when you bound and carried off Zechariah and Jehial and Claudius, our brother from Philippi. When you attacked the believers, you attacked our leader. The simple fact is, Jesus still lives—in us!"

A few years later, Reuel and I moved to Ephesus to be near our grandchildren. Thankfully I can say the Lord has enabled me to forgive Saul (who now is called Paul). His conversion was really genuine, and we rejoice in the miracle God has worked in the life of one who had so affected our lives.

On a certain Sunday morning we had gathered for worship with other Christians. There was special excitement because the church had received a wonderful epistle from Paul, and we had been reading portions from it week by week. On this day we read a passage that had special significance for me as I reflected on my days of praying for Reuel in prison. "Now to him who is able to do immeasurably more than all we ask or imagine, according to his power that is at work within us, to him be glory in the church and in Christ Jesus throughout all generations, for ever and ever! Amen."

Thank you, Lord, for your power that so clearly sustained us during those days. And thank you that you even revealed yourself to that young man, and now you're using him so effectively. Once he attacked us; now he is a blessing to us.

I couldn't resist a nudge. I grinned at Reuel (a favor he returned), leaned over, and whispered, "When you think of what we've been through with Jesus, you can't help but love him, can you?"

Acts 7:54–8:3; 9:1–9; Ephesians 3:20–21

FOR REFLECTION: What aspects of my life need to be impacted by the radical truth that Jesus Christ dwells within me?

CHAPTER TWENTY-ONE

IMAGINE STAYING WITH HIM FOREVER

Sitting here with pen in hand, I realize I'm up against more than the periodic "writer's block," the mental logjam that inhibits the verbal flow downstream. Instead, I confront the unenviable task of molding earthly words to describe a life in another, unearthly dimension.

Scratch "unenviable." Insert "impossible."

I suppose the impossibility of the endeavor is itself evidence that living with Jesus forever will be blessedly different than anything we could possibly now experience. It will take new words to explain, new minds to understand. It will mean having a place prepared especially for us, a home with our God who knows us each by name.

Do you share my frustration?

I hope so, for it means you're a candidate for reunion. Blessed are they with logjams of the heart, for they will see Jesus.

ARISE, COME!

Would you like to hear a story of love and heroism?

Once upon an eternity, there was a prince who fell in love. He wanted his beloved to care for him by her own choice, not out of admiration for his royalty. So he went to her dressed as a common man and set about to court her affections. He wooed her lovingly and with honor. Finally he won her betrothal.

But there was a complication. Her life was in mortal danger at the hands of a wicked villain who wanted her for himself. She was helpless to save herself from the overpowering evil of her destructive suitor. So her beloved did the only thing that could save her: He gave his life in exchange for hers.

Instantly her life was a mixture of the bittersweet. While moved beyond words by the sacrificial devotion of her prince, she was struck by the all-consuming loss of her first and only love. She saw no way of living any longer. She despaired of life; then suddenly he reappeared to her from the dead.

The prince told his beloved that he must go away for a time, promising to prepare a place for her while he was away, that one day he would return and bring her there to live with him.

They pledged their loyalty to one another and departed. In her betrothed's absence, she longed deeply for him. She kept herself only for him, refusing to play the harlot or to give herself to any of the suitors who sought to win her affection. *My lover is mine, and I am his. Many waters cannot quench love; rivers cannot wash it away.*

Her prince seemed to stay away for so very long. She wondered at times what had happened to him and if he really planned to return after such a long time. Yet in hope she continued to wait for him alone. Unexpectedly one day her prince came for her privately.

"Arise, my darling, my beautiful one, and come with me.
    See! The winter is past; the rains are over and gone.
    Flowers appear on the earth; the season of singing has come,
    the cooing of doves is heard in our land.
The fig tree forms its early fruit;
    the blossoming vines spread their fragrance.
Arise, come, my darling; my beautiful one, come with me."

Then, just as suddenly, there was a mighty shout and the piercing sound of wedding trumpets from beyond the mountaintops. All who heard it were amazed, not knowing the meaning of the alarm. They looked, and before long the answer was clear: The prince had come unexpectedly for his bride, and they had eloped together!

Many could not believe they had missed their opportunity to partake in such a blessed event. The courtship of the ages had happened right under their noses, and they had discarded their invitations to the wedding of all weddings.

The marriage supper was unparalleled. Such celebration, such music by thousands of choirs, such food never before tasted by the bride. It was delightful to her beyond telling. *Like an apple tree among the trees of the forest is my lover among the young men. I delight to sit in his shade, and his fruit is sweet to my taste. He has taken me to the banquet hall, and his banner over me is love. Strengthen me with raisins, refresh me with apples, for I am faint with love.* But the suddenness of his coming had left the bride without a chance to prepare herself completely. She felt that her clothing was inadequate for this grand occasion—until she looked down at herself and discovered that somehow she had been transformed. She could hardly believe her eyes, for she now wore the most brilliantly white gown ever seen, made of the finest white linen. It was adorned with jewels and all manner of exquisite lace, with a long and purely elegant train.

Then, in all this glory, she was presented for all to see: She came down from heaven, adorned for her husband. She was a bride in her youth and beauty, without spot or wrinkle. Her groom looked at her and saw faithfulness and holiness, for she pleased him now in every way. He wiped away every tear from her eyes, and all regret was gone. She would never know pain or mourning or death again.

For all her beauty, it was nevertheless the groom who was the central figure of the wedding. Everyone in attendance knew that it was he who had sought and won her. The prince had given his very life to rescue her. The bride basked in the greater glory of her husband.

Theirs was the first honeymoon that never ended. Neither had a job to return to. They required no hotel reservations, for the whole kingdom belonged to them. They had no quarrels or arguments to bring them back to earth. Their only task was to enjoy one another forever.

The only thing left to tell is the matter of their Father. Never fear that he might have been in any way jealous of the attention focused on the lovely pair. He couldn't have been any more delighted. In fact, it could probably be said that no one enjoyed the occasion more than he, for no one loves a beautiful wedding more than a successful Matchmaker!

Song of Songs 2:3–17; Ephesians 5:25–27; 1 Thessalonians 4:13–18; Revelation 19:6–9; 21:1–4

FOR REFLECTION: Is my manner of waiting in concert with his manner of devotion?

ROLL-CALL GLITCH

"All right, everybody." The archangel had a job on his hands. "You're all being so patient. Why, it's heavenly...excuse the pun. But bear with me: We're trying to locate at least one representative of the last tribe to hear the gospel and enter the kingdom."

Everyone understood the importance of this discovery and knew that the Lord of the harvest could not have made a mistake. It was only a matter of logistics. Finding one person in the masses of heaven was no small feat, especially with the spontaneous reunions that ignited the place with joy.

Michael continued, "Let's go about this in an organized fashion. Those of you who lived during earth's last half-century, listen up and pass the word around. If you prayed that the Lord would open doors for the Good News to reach peoples and tribes that had not heard it in a way they could understand, please identify yourself."

The response was astounding. Thousands of brothers and sisters from every continent raised their hands. A great cheer of appreciation went up.

But the number responding was so great it hardly narrowed the field of investigation. "Now, where are you who helped teach young people the importance of fulfilling the Great Commission?"

After another widespread indication, Michael stayed on the trail. "How many parents do we have here who released their children as missionaries?" A jubilant band, scattered among the multitudes but strangely united, shouted out their presence. The archangel acceded to the crowd's desire to applaud. At his signal the brethren roared their gratitude.

"Now, let's get right to the heart of the matter. Could we see the missionaries who brought the news of Christ to the unreached peoples of the world?"

It was an elite troop, not as many as you might have expected.

One among them, Thomas by name, moved toward the front. "I was sent to the tribe you're searching for. And I succeeded in finding them."

"Wonderful!" said the angel. "Do you remember who responded to the Good News?"

"Of course! How could I forget? He was a small man. Had the most infectious smile after he found Jesus. When I met him, he was traveling home to his village with two cows. He..."

"You mean me?" All eyes turned and looked in the direction of the sonorous voice. Everyone focused on a small person, smile intact. "Is that you, Thomas? I knew you'd be here somewhere."

Michael sensed that his puzzle was finally solved.

The sonorous voice continued, "Sorry for the confusion, everyone. I heard all the investigations going on. I just couldn't imagine that you would be talking about me and my tribe."

This struck most people as a bit humorous. Chuckles rippled about as he continued, "I wasn't unreached. Fact is, I had already started praying for an open door to the tribe over the hill. That's why I raised my hand with the first group!"

Celebration punctuated his sentence.

Thomas spoke up again. "No kidding! That's wonderful. But they already had the gospel. In fact, they're represented here too."

"That's right, we're here too," sounded several voices.

Just then the discussion was upstaged. You could hear it building from the distance—a new song focusing the attention where everyone wanted it to be:

"You are worthy to take the scroll and to open its seals,

because you were slain, and with your blood
you purchased men for God
from every tribe and language and people and nation.
You have made them to be a kingdom and priests to serve our God,
and they will reign on the earth."

As they sang, their words emphasized "You are worthy." Their smiles emphasized "every tribe"!

Revelation 5:9–10
FOR REFLECTION: Isn't it incredible to consider that not one group of people will be unaccounted for? What part can I play in making this so?

SIMPLY SPEECHLESS

I found myself standing before the man who, at one and the same time, was my Rescuer and my King.

Incredible and irresistible waves of love and adoration crashed on the shore of my soul. To my delight, I was before the throne of the one I cherished! All I wanted was to please him, to give myself to him fully and completely as an expression of my wonder.

But I couldn't.

I couldn't speak. Couldn't sing, couldn't write. I found no way within me to communicate my undying affection.

I didn't feel condemned for this. There was love, acceptance, and sympathy from all around me, even from my King. Yet I felt a deep ache in my spirit, for I was unable to share what I was dying to express.

Another person stepped forward. I could see that she held the same feelings for the Master as I did. I watched to see if she would have the same problem. At first she did. She tried to speak but to no avail. Flustered for a moment, she realized there was something she *could* do. She knelt down and placed before him an object she held in her hands. It was a gold chunk, the largest and most wonderfully brilliant piece I could imagine existed, not like any gold I had ever seen.

The sight of it brought magnificent joy to the King's face. He blessed her for what she had done.

And my heart sank lower. How envious I was. I too loved him, but I had no way of saying it. My hands were empty.

Then another person stepped forward. He, too, discovered that his only way of expressing his worship was to place at the Master's feet the object he carried, a large and lustrous gem, so resplendent it seemed as if light emanated from the stone itself.

A nearby attendant must have seen the consternation on my face. He came to me and said, "The first woman you saw used to quietly visit orphans and widows. She received the gold as a reward. The man you observed decided to follow the Master under very difficult circumstances. He was raised in Islam and was ostracized from his family for the sake of Christ."

Others continued to come before the King, placing exquisite crowns and varieties of sparkling gems before him. During their lives they had been humble in spirit, some serving in noticeable ways, others very unobtrusively.

"That man," the attendant continued, "refused to take sides when a spirit of division swept through his church. That woman prayed faithfully for thirty years without result for a friend's salvation. That one was a famous preacher who championed the truth, preaching faithfully and resisting many temptations for women and wealth." All, it seemed to me, had labored in their own ways to bring glory to Christ Jesus, many in little-known ways. But now, the King's brilliance illuminated them beyond comparison; they were now great lights and would have all eternity to reflect Christ's glory.

I noticed I wasn't the only one feeling helpless. Others stood beside and behind me, simply watching as I was, unable to voice their praise. They, too, had nothing to give.

One had served in a very visible ministry for Christ, but she had done it for her own honor. Most of the others were obviously surprised, having expected to have more to show for their Christian lives. But their works, like mine, had burned up like dry twigs in the firestorm of his righteous gaze. We had nothing left to offer him.

No one argued with his judgment. He was perfect righteousness. The selfish motives behind our works were laid bare. There was no debate. Only regret.

I thought of all the times I attended worship meetings with my heart remote and uninvolved. Now I had the most intense desire to worship, but I couldn't! I had not lived so as to possess the currency for praise. I had thought I was rich but found instead that I was bankrupt, smothered under the counterfeit coins of self-centeredness.

Have you ever known the ecstasy of realizing, upon waking up, that your plight was only a dream? Have you ever found in that ecstasy a deep motivation to change your part in the story?

I have. And when it happened to me, I determined not to meet Christ empty-handed.

Matthew 5:3–12; 6:19–21; 1 Corinthians 3:7–15; 2 Corinthians 5:10
FOR REFLECTION: I have the firm foundation. What am I building on it?

A GLIMPSE

I hesitate to tell the story for fear of being written off as one who has bidden farewell to his senses. But tell it I must. It's an experience too unbelievable to be real, yet too real to be imagined. And too important to be left untold.

You see, I took a long journey, but I'm not actually sure if I went anywhere. It was a pilgrimage upward....

On this journey I see sights I've never before seen: high soaring birds, clouds shrinking down to white patches below. Eventually I enter the cold and darkness of open space where uncounted galaxies emerge from the blackness.

There is, as if overlaid, another dimension which I had previously only heard about: worlds of spirit beings of all kinds and sizes. Some have a horrific look about them, filled with hatred and deceit...ugliness beyond description so that I bristle with fear.

But others emanate strength, kindness, and truth. I'm among the angels.

As I proceed upward, the levels of spirit beings increase in dimension and might. Their clashes against each other become more fierce. I see Falsehood fighting Truth. I dearly want to help Truth, but a dimension separates me from the struggle. My powerlessness frustrates me. I wish that God would do something. I yearn that the Spirit of Jesus might intervene.

Then I see a truthful being prevail over his adversary, and he nods approvingly at me. *I wonder why. Did I do something?*

By and by I begin to hear singing, glorious singing. Light begins to grow, and before long its increasing brilliance forces me to shield my eyes. I feel a powerful Presence—familiar but nearer than ever before. But I can't seem to get any closer. I have no one to guide me, for by now I've passed above all counselors. As I consider what to do, the Spirit reminds me of the way. So I look and look for it.

My search is rewarded by the discovery of a narrow but open door which leads to a passageway. Because of the brightness, which I cannot even approach, I squint to see anything that marks my way in. As I do so, I begin to make out an image, indistinct at first. I move toward it, upward and in, straining to make out its shape. I begin to see that it actually consists of two forms, one just like the other. Suddenly it becomes clear. They are two feet.

Two nail-scarred feet.

I embrace them. And wish for a vial of perfume.

Then I notice, almost as an observer of myself, that a transformation has occurred. The light no longer hurts my eyes. And I'm singing...gloriously singing! (I who used to produce as much music as a stone!) We sing and sing and sing of his Name.

Upward, there is a huge host. Singing. Laughing. Conversing. Learning. Honoring and being honored. Each in a mansion of his own, but somehow all intertwined, as if in one body.

For a moment my viewpoint changes. Instead of looking at this host, I am a part of it, looking out from a place that fits me perfectly, for it is my own. I feel tremendous joy and power flowing down. Love binds me wonderfully with all those around me, whom I now know by name.

I look farther up, for I know this fountain of love washing through me has a Source. I know who it is, but I just want to see him. *Just a glimpse. One...little...glimpse.*

And I do see him.

There, above the scar of the spear. There, laced by the healed pockmarks of the thorns. It's his face. He smiles at me, one on one, and I realize as never before the joy of being in Christ.

And it is enough.

To be sure, I want to stay. Stay forever, right here. And stay I will.

But I realize that, for now, this is but a taste, a peek. I know instinctively that I must return and live in the light of what I've seen.

And in a way, I want to do this. For I see now the glory of scars. I want them on my own body. I want to seize the authority of his Name, above every rule and power. I want to live in the warmth of his smile and remember how fully he fills.

And then, after a few short years, I'll be back this instant.

2 Corinthians 12:1–10; Ephesians 1:18–23

FOR REFLECTION: How can I live today now that I've glimpsed eternal reality?

EPILOGUE

As we end this leg of the journey, my prayer for you is identical to my prayer for myself:

May you live your life
in such a way
that when you meet him face to face
you won't even need
an introduction.

SCRIPTURE INDEX

Scripture Index, cont.

INDEX OF BIBLICAL CHARACTERS